In 1717 a governing authority known as the "Grand Lodge of England" was established at a meeting of four surviving lodges in the Apple Tree Tavern in London. Two Protestant clergymen, Dr. John Theophilus Desaguliers and Dr. James Anderson, were instrumental in setting up the self-styled governing body. Not all lodges were willing to submit to the rule of the new Grand Lodge, but by 1725 the original four lodges had grown to sixty four, of which fifty were in London. The Craft captured the fancy of certain members of the English aristocracy after 1721, and they in turn were flattered by the brethren. The first royal Grand Master took office in that year, and this position has since then been reserved to a nobleman.

-*Christianity and American Freemasonry*, William J. Whalen

The Apple-Tree
Art and Knowledge of the Craft

SPRING 2010   Volume I: Issue 1

Edited by and cover art by Brother Tommy Baas, Freemasons Lodge 363, Milwaukee, WI

Art, essays, poetry, etc., always welcome. Please submit all contributions to gnostictom@yahoo.com

"Don't tell me there are no designs on the Trestleboard..."

The Light of Morn
by Brother Tom Curtis

The beauty
Of the light of morn,
Tinged with yellow
And green pastels,
Calls to me
Like some winged bird
Of paradise
With its subtle hues
Singing of friendships
Long ago.
Sadness and joy
Are equal mixed,
With those soft thoughts
Brought home and joined
With friendships yet to be,
Within our Craft.
It is a symphony
Of Life
So rich
That the soul
Can scarcely take it in,
The Architect's gift
To you and me,
The gift of Love.

April Is The Reverse October
by Brother David White

Percussive wind
White fossils blowing off sand
Moon sits low
Saturn is high
Listen now the motion
of howling winds roaring the
rage and the lows
Lakes send back lunar aftermath

Humble
by Brother David White

We wait for sun
We watch the moon
We cast fires
For those long gone
Our hearts remember them
Our tears water flowers
Flowers need this
We need this
It keeps us humble
Passing through thicket and forest
The presence of light remains to remind us
all is not lost
The presence of light is near again
Move with the knowledge every breath
and every vision is a blessed one

Genetic Conference
by Brother David White

Burn away dust and rock
Stars and comets shed their bodies
and become new boys and girls
falling to Earth
and as they arrive here mothers and fathers
wrap them in warm blankets
and pray for their happiness

Mysteries of the Craft

Join **Freemasons Lodge 363**'s stated meeting on **Wednesday, May 5** at 5:30pm in the Humphrey Scottish Rite Masonic Temple for a presentation by **Brother David J. White** on the science and symbolic philosophy of Alchemy as it relates to Freemasonry.

in a moment's alchemy
by Brother Tommy Baas

life apart from dreaming becomes
the struggle of idealizing
reality and realizing the ideal
without losing the fluid self in material pomp

time free me of these long days
and let me sleep with an open book over my face
i am only so far removed
from my element
conceived angelic
i have seen the sprig of acacia and know
that i know what i know
that the religions of man
are the artful mindgames of God
and earth the childbride of liquid fire
dancing

Color Scheme
by Brother Tommy Baas

I have a lamb
I want to give the world
her name is Hope
her home the Third Temple
the old lady
her maintaining pleasure in life
the weeding of her personal garden
when only time is in vain
and the front porch a windy-heighted perch
on the mast of still perspective

Zerubbabel: Master Mason to the Second Temple

by Brother Tommy Baas

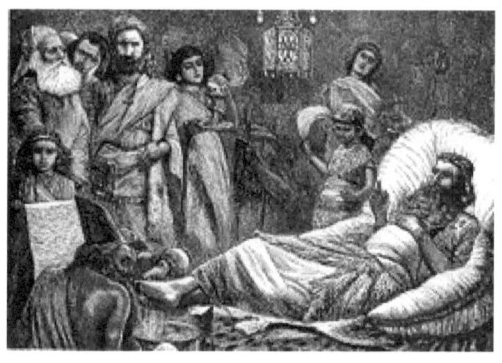

Familiar to Scottish Rite Masons through the 15th and 16th Degrees of the Princes of Jerusalem is a name we all love to pronounce, if we can only get it right, belonging to a great Jewish patriarch who we might consider a sort of secondary hero of Masonic legend. After all Zerubbabel is to the Second Temple who Hiram Abif is to the first Temple of Solomon. Both figures were esteemed as especially wise and skilled builders in Phoenicia and were responsible for the building of the foundations of the respective Temples of Jerusalem. As Masonic icons, both are revered for exemplifying profound dignity in ensuring the temple be built with the utmost integrity to the secrets of Freemasonry. What secrets Hiram in the 3rd Degree allegory protects even against threats on his life, Zerubbabel protects the same in the 15th Degree against the temptation of riches and the return of the Temple's most sacred, yet material, furniture. In the 16th Degree, the idolatrous ways of the three members of King Darius's court who debate over what holds the most powerful sway over man could symbolically be likened to that of the three ruffians who conspired against Hiram in the 3rd Degree. Esoterically, such might reflect the three conceptual negative forces of Nature, or man's threefold lower nature, in direct opposition to the more positive forces, epitomized in Christianity's Holy Trinity and characterized as Hiram Abif, Hiram King of Tyre, and King Solomon (and perhaps also as Zerrubabel, Joshua the Priest, and Haggai the Prophet).

Zerubbabel is to the Second Temple who Hiram Abif is to the first Temple of Solomon

---

While there are but two minor mentions of Hiram in the Old Testament and none in either the New Testament or any Gnostic or other Apocryphal texts, we have as sources for the life of Zerubbabel: the genealogies of two Synoptic gospels from the New Testament, the book of Ezra from the Old Testament, the Aprocyphal text I Esdras, the works of the great Jewish scholar Josephus Flavius, and various old Masonic rituals compiled and filtered through by Christopher Knight and Robert Lomas into what they call "The Masonic Testament" (*The Book of Hiram*).

Several texts explicitly state Zerubbabel to be the son of Shealtiel, but the genealogy in I Chronicles explicitly refers to him as the son of Pedaiah (3:19), making him a nephew to Shealtiel. Whatever the case, he was apparently the Prince of Judah. He is commonly associated with the name Sheshbazzar, though there is speculation that this name may refer to the character who gained permission under Cyrus to rebuild the Temple and that it was Zerubbabel who re-established this decree under Darius, whereas the texts otherwise seem to depict the two personages as one and the same. Perhaps an elusive distinction might exist? According to Matthew, Zerubbabel (here spelled "Zorobabel") was the 11th ancestor from Jesus, whereas according to Luke, he was the 20th. While even the Synoptics aren't always completely synoptic, we at least know that Zerubbabel was a leading descendent of the House of David by the Tribe of Judah. A strong and skilled Pheonician artificer of the Dionysian Mysteries, Hiram was of the notoriously pagan-like Tribe of Naphtali through his widowed mother, whose old man was the great Jewish patriarch, Ur. As in the case of Jesus, Hiram's mixed origins set him at controversy among the Jews (in Hiram's case, the "Juwes"), who would jealously conspire the hero's demise, insisting that one whose blood and/or beliefs might not be purely orthodox should not be fit to furnish the Temple of Jerusalem (Brown, John W., "Hiram Abiff"). Zerubbabel, as he proclaims in the 15th Degree, and as we can discern from genealogies connecting him with both Jesus and King Solomon, was of the Tribe of Judah. Now *Judah* we know of as the son of Jacob (aka, Israel) who suggested selling his brother Joseph out to the Egyptians, similar to how *Judas* (the Greek derivation of *Judah*) infamously sold his brother Jesus out to the Romans. The story of Joseph told in the 12th Degree of Scottish Rite Masonry follows more or less faithfully the same story told in Genesis. Esoterically, as the "Lion of Israel," Judah, or Judas, represents the zodiacal house of Leo, through which the Sun (anthropomorphized by Joseph with his brilliantly-colored coat in the O.T. and by Jesus with his setting and rising in the N.T.) passes before it is "crucified," or brought to a low point for "three days" (similarly reflected in the three Craft degrees) before resurrecting again anew. This "low point" of darkness is allegorized in various ways throughout the Bible, either as slavery, death (in a more spiritual sense than necessarily physical), or hell. On another esoteric level, this "darkness" represents the human body in which the Logos or the Light of the Holy Spirit is entombed at physical birth, before it is resurrected by spiritual re-birth through initiatory rites such as Masonry and the Ancient Mysteries practice.

Before the building of the First Temple, this place of darkness was symbolized as Egypt. In the Book of Genesis we find this phenomenon of Light being shadowed by and subsequently rising up from Darkness, portrayed in the exile in Egypt out of which Moses led his Exodus, and also in the same Egypt where Joseph spent his slavery before being placed at the *right hand of the king* where he preached *forgiveness*. Further similar to both Moses and Joseph, Jesus in the New Testament also speaks of rising up out of Egypt.

The very name Zerubbabel refers to one conceived in Babylon

For rituals and allegories concerning the building of the Second Temple, the land of captivity out of which the hero leads his people has become Babylon. The very name Zerubbabel refers to one conceived in Babylon, a.k.a., Babel. Some Masonic origin theories suggest that the descendents of Nimrod, being ancestral Freemasons, were responsible for erecting that notorious Tower of Babel (Mackey, *The History of Freemasonry*, pg. 59), which, as punishment for mankind blasphemously building a temple to God by idolatrous means, resulted in the one universal language being confounded into a million tongues and the building being destroyed. This confounding of the universal language into a myriad of confused tongues can be likened to the substituting of the Master's Word or the Ineffable Name into various words and names only able to capture disjointedly aspects of God's glory (for such is the inherent fallibility of language and such human efforts when attempting to describe the divine...hence the True Word being wholly ineffable). And the selfish sins of the people are often blamed in Jewish legend for the destruction of sacred temples and subsequent exiles. Indeed this idea is reflected in Haggai's prophesy which Joshua throws in Zerubabel's face in the opening scene of the 16th Degree. "Being preoccupied with building our own houses and neglecting the Temple" is synonymous with general idolatry in the language of the Western Mysteries. Similar was the reason given for the Great Flood against which Noah built his ark by God's instruction. It is against this so human nature which our heroes Hiram and Zerubbabel must fight with courageously unflinching dedication if the erection of the temple is to by won with integrity enough to sustain its walls against both the weapons of its enemies and the greed of its own people. Jesus got busy knocking over tables and scattering coins when the idolatry of the money-lenders threatened to blaspheme the sacristy of the Temple. In the 16th Degree, the characteristically human suggestions that the king, wine, and women each might yield the most powerful sway over man constitute idolatry unbecoming to the Lord of Truth. But as we'll see, the text of I Esdras, when compared to our 16th Degree script, might reveal an interesting twist on Zerubbabel's position on the matter, and could even further muddy the question of his seemingly split identity.

Let us now trace Zerubbabel's story, as pieced together by our various sources. We begin at the end of the Exile, Nebuzaradan having destroyed Jerusalem and put the remaining Jews to work in Babylon. The land of Judah is all that remains of the kingdom of Jerusalem, but the new king of the region receives Jeremiah's prophesy that one shall come who is worthy to restore the city and its temple to the Jewish god. End II Chronicles, begin the book of Ezra. In 538 B.C., Cyrus, king of Persia, captures Babylon, making him master of an empire stretching from the Caspian Sea to the Mediterranean. From there he sought conquest of Egypt, to which end it became to his strategic advantage to repatriate to Jerusalem the Jews who had under the previous regime been deported to Babylon and to dub them allies of his court. In the first chapter of Ezra, it is mentioned that Cyrus hands the vessels of the old temple which had been ransacked by Nebuchadnezzar over to Sheshbazzar, here referred to as the Prince of Judah, who then brings these vessels to those Jews brought up from Babylonian captivity. Could these be the same sacred vessels with which Zerubbabel is tempted in the 15th Degree? The very next chapter of Ezra has Zerubbabel leading the released children of Israel unto Judah, as granted according to Cyrus's decree.

The land of Judah is all that remains of the kingdom of Jerusalem, but the new king of the region receives Jeremiah's prophesy that one shall come who is worthy to restore the city and its temple to the Jewish god.

In the Masonic Testament made up of old degrees compiled by Knight and Lomas, Cyrus directly connects Sheshbazzar the Prince of Judah with Zerubbabel, who waits outside as the king regales his prophetic dream to his knights and guards. In our 15th Degree, it is Daniel, a Jewish exile kept as a court vizier through the Chaldean occupation (and apparently an old friend of Zerubbabel's), who interprets the king's dream. The details of the dream seem to loosely correspond to visions revealed in the Book of Daniel, at least to the extent that they (a) foreshadow the redemption of the Jewish people from exile and the restoration of the House of the Lord, and (b) symbolically utilize one or more of the four apocalyptic beasts of Ezekial's vision, also symbolical of the Four Elements and associated with the four Evangelists attributed with the authorship of the four respective gospels. Of these four creatures, the Ox, Lion, Eagle, and Man, it is the Lion, perhaps because representative of the Tribe of Judah, who takes a particularly prominent role in the king's dream. The Lion is also of course significant both with Solomon and the grip the king uses to raise up Hiram Abiff, the Layer of the Foundation of the First Temple on the brow of Mount Moriah. Supposedly Solomon chose this spot near Jerusalem, having preferred it to the site of Enoch's old temple, whose ruins he mistook to be heathen and thus marking a desecrated spot. But it was from these ruins that Hiram would find the fabled refused stone which would become the head corner stone of the Temple. When Hiram's mutilated remains are found and raised up by Solomon's grip of the Lion's Paw, they are reburied "on the brow of a hill, West of Mount Moriah." It would seem these remains would provide the foundation stone of the Second Temple.

One of the more popular visions of the Book of Daniel pits the prophet in the Lion's Den for disobeying King Darius's edict not to worship anyone, god or human, but his own sovereignty. Finding Daniel blameless before Him and faithful even against the king's edict, the God of Israel sends his angel to shut up the lion's mouth so it did not hurt him, reminiscent of the Eighth Arcana of the Tarot, that of Strength. In slight variation yet still faithful to intent, Cyrus's vision as interpreted by Daniel pits the lion against the king if he refuses to restore Jerusalem to its exiled people and their fathers' god. Trying to follow the whole legend using the books of Daniel, Ezra, and Esdras and the actual historical account of Josephus seems to present a bit of a disjointed lineage in kingship, which could perhaps be chalked up to visionary whims and textual digressions. In the Book of Daniel, the story of the lion's den involving a king Darius, referred to as a Mede, follows the death of Belshazzar (son of Nebuchadnezzer), the Chaldean king (not to be mistaken with Belteshazzar, who Daniel himself is dubbed by King Cyrus later on in the Book of Daniel). This Darius the Mede who pits Daniel in the lion's den is said at the end of Chapter 5 to have taken up the reign at age 62 after Belshazzar is killed, purportedly for his sacrilege, fulfilling Daniel's prophetic interpretation of the same king's dream. No such person as Darius the Mede is known to historical record; though Persia yielded three kings named Darius, the King Darius important to the 16th Degree succeeds Cambyses II, heir to King Cyrus. It was Cyrus whose edict overthrew the Neo-Babylonian power (Ezra 1:1), almost "ten weeks of years" (70 years) after Daniel's coming to Babylon. Interestingly Cyrus had a general named Gobyras who was about 62 years-old when he occupied Babylon. And complicated discrepancies regarding kinship, marriage, and children would seem to credit this Gobyras and a man named Darius with descendents by the same woman, if the two are not indeed one and the same man. According to the chronology followed by the author of the Book of Daniel, the first year of Darius the Mede would fall on 538 B.C., the very year King Cyrus began his reign.

Daniel's prophesies in the Book of Daniel would seem to correspond fairly enough with his prophetic interpretation of Cyrus's dream as recounted in the 15th Degree. The gist of his visions draws fatal punishment to those kings (particularly Nebuchadnezzer and Belshezzar) who would desecrate the kingdom to sacrilege and greed rather than allow the Jews to restore their city and temple to their god, and warns Cyrus and his successors of the same if they not heed the Lord's wishes. Daniel and his prophesies are not actually mentioned in the Book of Ezra, which covers the reign of the four kings beginning with Cyrus, which period would yield the return of Jerusalem from Babylonian captivity. Nor are they mentioned in I Esdras, an apocryphal text which reproduces the substance of II Chronicles, the whole of Ezra, and part of Nehemiah, all with minor discrepancies and one significant addition, not found in any other biblical texts, which tells the story regaled in the 16th Degree.

The people of Judah were constantly harassed and discouraged from their efforts to rebuild throughout the reign of Cyrus and until the reign of Darius

Verses 4:7-23 of Ezra and correspondingly 2:16-30 of I Esdras presents either a chronologically premature digression or a confusion over the name of the residing king. Just before this passage in Ezra, it is mentioned that the people of Judah were constantly harassed and discouraged from their efforts to rebuild throughout the reign of Cyrus and until the reign of Darius. The passage in question tells of a letter of complaint to King Artaxerxes written by those insisting upon the thwarting of such efforts by the Jewish people, on the grounds that Jerusalem had previously proved hostile to kingdoms that did not recognize their god. For such was the very reason for the destruction of the Jewish Temple in the first place. According to the passage, King Artaxerxes issues a decree in response to this complaint, ordering the work of the Israelites to cease, which it subsequently does "until the second year of the reign of King Darius of Persia." Of course the reign of King Artaxerxes I (465-424 B.C.) *follows after* the reign of his father Xerxes I (485 – 465), who was the son of King Darius (521-485). If this passage were simply misplaced, it should follow chronologically between the Book of Ezra and that of Nehemiah. But the line "until…Darius" and the fact that the temple was completed under his reign betrays more likely an issue of mixed identities, an issue which indeed seems all too common to our study. It was Cambyses II (529-521), the son of Cyrus (538-529), who preceded Darius and attempted to overturn his father's decree protecting the efforts of the returned Jews, and Josephus provides this correction (*Ant.* XI. ii.1-3). The modern ritual of the 16th Degree gets this right, but Albert Pike's earlier version of the same errantly refers to Artaxerxes as the king who frustrates the efforts of the Jews (*The Magnum Opus or The Great Work*). Both Cyrus and Darius were disciples of Zoroaster and worshipped God as a unified One, thus were their religious views compatible with the Jews' through the common ground of Freemasonry, in the same respect that the different faiths of King Solomon, Hiram King of Tyre, and Hiram Abiff were reconciled into one symbolic Mystery language.

In the 15th Degree, it is for Zerubbabel's unflinching faithfulness in keeping the secrets of Freemasonry, even when tempted by Cyrus's offer to return the First Temple's most prized relics to the Jewish people, that he is rewarded privilege in the court and permission to rebuild the city of Jerusalem and its temple. Considering Cyrus's military agenda, as stated previously, such a decree would be to his advantage anyway, though his heir would see things differently. This might explain why Zerubbabel is made a knight of the court and given a sword, with instructions to make more knights of his friends whom he found fit. Cyrus seemed to want to make an allied army of the Jews. It is also at this point that Cyrus bestows to Zerubbabel from his treasury the sacred vessels and relics belong to the First Temple; the same which he does for "Sheshbazzar" according to Ezra, which designation is apparently the Baylonian name of a Jewish court official.

Cyrus seemed to want to make an allied army of the Jews.

In their Masonic Testament, Knight and Lomas provide us with details from old Royal Arch Degrees which would seem to fall chronologically between the events of the 15th Degree and those of the 16th Degree. Having gained permission from Cyrus to rebuild the temple, Zerubbabel organizes a Grand and Royal Lodge of Babylon from his compatriots for the direction of the work and the conferring of degrees. This was done much in the same manner that Hiram organized his guild for the erection of the First Temple, except using various degrees familiar to the Scottish and York Rites rather than the three degrees of Craft Masonry. A small group of three Masons came seeking permission from this Grand Lodge that they might assist in the rebuilding of the Temple. Zerubbabel brought these three sojourners into the Council Chamber, enquiring from whence they came. A Craft Mason answers such a question that he has travelled from West to East and then back West again, and when asked why he left the East, the source of Light, he answers that he went out "in search of that which was lost." When asked if he found such, the Craft Mason answers that he "did not, but found a substitute." To Zerubbabel's question, these three Masons answer that they have travelled from Babylon, the land of captivity, and when asked why the left the same and came to Jerusalem, the city of promise, the three reply that they wish to assist in rebuilding the Temple. In the respective allegories, East is Jerusalem; West is either Egypt or Babylon. When asked how they hoped to obtain such admission, their answer is not dissimilar to that of the Craft Mason who seeks further Light through the proceeding degrees: "by virtue of certain signs, tokens and words." By the proof of these means, the three Masons are recognized as worthy brothers and admitted into the lodge to assist with the work.

Zerubbabel sends the three Masons out to task with the particular injunction that should they in the course of their work happen upon any relics belonging to the old Temple, they will immediately report the same unto the Council Chamber. The very next day, the three Masons present themselves before Zerubbabel to report just such a discovery: a large brazen ring fixed to a broad flat stone engraved with certain letters familiar to the workers, alluding to hidden treasures. The stone was then raised to reveal the crown of a perfect arch. Not being able to find his way into it, the workman loosened the keystone with a crowbar which he drew forth to the discovery of a cavity beneath. Apprehensive of danger and foul air eerily similar to that which turned off the Fellowcraft at the site of Hiram's decomposing body in the 3rd Degree Allegory, the workmen cast lots to determine who should descend the cavity by means of a cable tow around his waist held on to above by his companions. Certain characters on the Keystone found revealed the cavity to be the secret vault of King Solomon known as the Sanctum Sanctorum, or Holy of Holies. Another stone was removed and another worker lowered down, who brought back up a roll which was discovered to be the Book of the Holy Law. Then a third stone was drawn, enlargening the opening, and yet another worker was lowered down. The sun was now at meridian height, marking that prayer time so favored by Hiram, and it became that much easier to see inside the vault. The Masonic Testament describes thus what the worker saw:

"On examining the place he found it to be a splendid apartment supported on seven pillars; round the architraves were the twelve signs of the Zodiac, and the names of the twelve tribes of Israel, and what had formerly been found, wrought into due and familiar form, proved on inspection to be an

Altar of pure white marble, in shape a double cube, and rich in sculptured ornaments, erected to the Lord God, for at that moment the meridian sun, darting his rays through the aperture, on top of the Altar, brilliantly illumined a circle of gold, on which was the grand, peculiar and mysterious name of Deity; and on a triangle of the same metal within the circle were inscribed other characters, of which they could not understand the meaning, although they did not doubt that they were connected with the Sacred Word itself."

The D and the Z at each side of the balancing sword in the symbol for the degrees of Princes of Jerusalem refer respectively to Darius and Zerubbabel

Having dutifully reported all that they had seen, the workers were sent back out by Zerubbabel, this time with Ezra the scribe, who was well-skilled in many languages. It is from him that we get the biblical account of Zerubbabel's adventures. He reports back to Solomon the veracity of the workers findings. Most significantly, Ezra finds the Jewel which belonged to Hiram Abiff at the base of the altar upon which the workers had found the initials of the three Grand Masters who had presided at the building of the First Temple. Incidentally, the D and the Z at each side of the balancing sword in the symbol for the degrees of Princes of Jerusalem refer respectively to Darius and Zerubbabel.

Naturally Zerubbabel is very impressed with these findings and bestows the workers with aprons, jewels, rods, and sashes. He explains that the mysterious characters on the triangle represent the name of God in three different languages, which all indicate the true and long-lost method of pronouncing the Sacred Word inscribed upon the circle. The Jewel bearing the mark of Hiram Abiff confirms the Masonic tradition that the ancient Master's Word which had been lost at the building of King Solomon's with Hiram's untimely death would one day be recovered, that the Temple, if destroyed, could be rebuilt to its full glory. For it is crux of Masonic faith that all that lives, lives forever, and all that is lost will be found again.

Now we come to the allegory of the 16th Degree, in the court of King Darius. Here is where the question is propounded for discussion as to what holds the most powerful sway over man. In an earlier version of this ritual, only the King, Beauty, and Truth are discussed as answers, and Zerubbabel suggests each of the latter two, ultimately giving Truth as his final answer. Rhetorically, Truth and Beauty are often associated by the old axiom, "Beauty is Truth." But Beauty is also often associated with Woman, and it is Women, rather than Beauty, which in I Esdras and the modern version of the ritual makes for the third suggested answer before Truth is arrived at (the first being Wine, the second, the King). And just as in the earlier ritual Zerubbabel suggests both Beauty and Truth, our hero actually suggests both Women and Truth in I Esdras! This may come as a shock to Scottish Rite Masons who are used to Zerubbabel deriding the three suggestions of Wine, the King, and Woman as idolatrous. Is there perhaps an incongruency in the text of I Esdras? We do know that it had been added to, if not amended, and that this entire section is absent from where it would fall in the Book of Ezra, which entire text is included almost word for word in I Esdras.

Verse 4:13 states, "Then the third, who had spoken of women and truth (and this was Zerubbabel), began to speak:" Having gone so far as to explicitly attribute this statement to the Prince of Judah, the text of the argument goes on word for word as it appears in the modern 16th Degree, with one significant exception, and this seems to be where the modern script writers got the name Bartacus, to whom they attribute the lengthy argument for Women, here attributed to Zerubbabel immediately before at equal length he counters the same with an argument for Truth.

In our 15th Degree, the argument for Women, as spoken by Bartacus, ends stating how many have "perished, or stumbled, or sinned because of women." From the mouth of Zerubbabel in I Esdras, this line is followed by one more paragraph on the suggestion of Women. It includes an unflattering poke at the suggestion of the King, which should seem to insult Darius—the very riddler and jury here being appealed to—even more than Zerubbabel's later statement in his argument for Truth that "the King is unrighteous", were Darius not so disposed to and impressed by the Prince's so bold integrity. "Is not the king great in his power? Do not all lands fear to touch him? Yet I have seen him with Apame, the king's concubine, the daughter of the illustrious Bartacus; she would sit at the king's right hand and take the crown from the king's head and put it on her own, and slap the king with her left hand. At this the king would gaze at her with mouth agape. If she smiles at him, he laughs; if she loses temper with him, he flatters her, so that she may be reconciled to him. Gentlemen, why are not women strong, since they do such things?" (I Esdras 4:28-32)

"Is not the king great in his power? Do not all lands fear to touch him? Yet I have seen him with Apame, the king's concubine, the daughter of the illustrious Bartacus; she would sit at the king's right hand and take the crown from the king's head and put it on her own, and slap the king with her left hand. At this the king would gaze at her with mouth agape. If she smiles at him, he laughs; if she loses temper with him, he flatters her, so that she may be reconciled to him. Gentlemen, why are not women strong, since they do such things?" (I Esdras 4:28-32)

Immediately following this argument, verse 4:33 has the king and nobles looking at one another in bewilderment, just before Zerubbabel commences speaking about truth, though not without reiterating his stance on the strength of Women. It would almost seem that he is arguing for Women and Truth as hand in hand, were it not for his statement that "Women are unrighteous" (in the modern 15th Degree, the word "wicked" is used in place of "unrighteous"). Of course it is completely possible for something to hold a powerful sway over man *and* be unrighteous, and perhaps this could be why Zerubbabel first appeals to the argument for Women before insisting upon Truth as a yet better answer. But wait… my *New Oxford Annotated Bible with the Apocrypha* comes with a footnote to Zerubbabel's speech on Truth in verses 4:33-41, referring to it as "an *addition* to the original story probably made prior to the story's adaption to the Jewish author's purpose." And the editor of *The HarperCollins Study Bible: New Revised Standard Versio with the Apocryphal/Deuterocanonical Books* goes even further than the Oxford editor regarding verses 4:33-41: "This speech in praise of truth contains no ambivalence about its subject. 'Truth' is here not freedom from error but more like 'virtue'; it is the opposite of 'unrighteousness' (4.37, 39-40). It is hard to see any real argument in this speech that truth is 'strong'; there is a claim that it endures and prevails (4.38), but no evidence is brought forward. The speech about truth has not been well integrated into the story of the three-cornered contest, which apparently existed earlier in a version without Zerubbabel."

This latter footnote backs up the statement of the former that this passage was a later integration, and an awkward one at that, but also suggests that the earlier version of the story *apparently* did not even include Zerubbabel. We can only guess as to what "apparent" implication might have led the editor to this conclusion; the parenthetical attribution of the Woman argument to Zerubbabel can be read as either explicit or suspicious. Perhaps the modern 15th Degree corrects the text of I Esdras by dividing the attribution of the arguments for Women and Truth to two separate persons (making only the latter to be Zerubbabel's sentiments, and attributing the former to one who's name is dropped in the very argument? But that creates an inherent absurdity, unless Bartacus be schizophrenic, or the proponent for Woman be someone else all together). We have already established that the modern version of the degree does (though the earlier Pike version of the degree does not) corrects an identity error in I Esdras where Cambyses II should be mentioned instead of Artaxerxes.

Verse 4:42 picks up with Darius commending and rewarding Zerubbabel for giving the correct answer to the riddle, though no reiteration is made by the king as to what that winning answer was. Zerubbabel seems to have made a rather lengthy and convincing argument for Women, which the following equally lengthy diatribe on Truth would seem to contradict. Indeed, were verses 4:33-41 left out all together, the story might run all the more smoothly. Perhaps even Zerubbabel's little anecdote about the king and his concubine might have blackmailed Darius's favor. Perhaps Woman was the right answer! In the original text, it would at least seem that Zerubbabel's final answer supports the sentiments of Harry Belafonte's song, "Man Smart, Woman Smarter." Does it follow that they do indeed hold the most powerful sway over man? The king's question did not specifically ask what is the most righteous, only what is the most powerful. And indeed, how often is a man swayed away by his lust for Woman, regardless of the influence of Truth?

Perhaps Woman was the right answer!

Elizabeth Aldworth Saint-Leger
The first Woman Freemason
Initiated 1712

Well, I've played the part of Bartacus my share of times in the 4th and 16th Degrees, and those who've seen me know how I really get into the role, and those who know me and my crazy dating track record know why I can relate to the role so well, maybe too well. But for as much as I seem to love complicated women, experience has tried to drill the profound lesson of the degree in to me again and again: Alas, there is *nothing* more powerful than **Truth!**

The Turtle Tarot

Created by Brother Tommy Baas

0 ~ The Fool

Before the first card, the Magician—or the initiate, is the candidate, the zero, out of which the first was formed. In the traditional version of the card, the dog at the Fool's left side is interpreted to be hostile, trying to bite the boy. I've felt that's either a yucky misinterpretation accepted over time or at least unbefitting of the feeling I personally got with the image. Naturally, Tommy is going to make the small dog to be the boy's affectionate companion.

    A prince by birthright, the prodigal son, having wandered off from his spoiled sense of security out of stubborn restlessness to experience the world and observe its laws and also the breaking of them and record his impressions in his journal (under right arm, with pen - the poet's magic wand), the fool peers longingly from atop a hill high, shedding tear for the heart (crying blood down the castle walls, as if out a bedroom window open) he craves back home at the castle where he belongs. He has only to descend the hill and cross the bridge. He is weary from travel, his jeans are ripped and he is barefoot. But the grass is green and it is full of red and yellow flowers which are soft to his feet. Being a prince by birthright, he never had to worry about security and having all needs met. So restless he went off to prove to himself that he could earn and deserve what had been given to him freely by the Grace of God. What he did was find Knowledge. He carries a small sack over his left arm and it carries his essential belongings, as he travels conservatively, so to make sure he can make it home if he has to. Like a turtle, he carries his home on his back. He has a hard shell and it is important for him to be strong, and as you can see by his flushed cheeks, the shame of Fallen Man which is the Cross carried, he is full of humbled adoration for the Lord and only wants to come before Him innocently. He is alone but for his dog and a dream. He carries a simple slingshot in his backpocket (though as a prince and a knight he's certainly entitled to carry a sword, he is modest and only means to protect) for he is like David to Goliath. ("He is an artist; he knows to create, not destroy" -a.b. 74 ;). He is a conservative, like his father. and uses only the resources he can carry, for what is most important is the journey, because at home is everything. He feels a fool for having strayed, yet is wise for it, and is also the wiser for wanting to return home really ready.

    He knows he cannot afford to be insecure or hasty. If he did not so firmly believe that he could make things better, he would not so firmly assert his wish; for that would be selfish egotism, whereas he Loves. He knows that poverty is not to be fancied a virtue but is modest about his riches. You do not see it because he doesn't show it-- he shares it. He does not live on credit, but work. He knows what's wrong with this world fallen as it is from Eden and is not afraid to sing about it. Some have interpreted the Fool as a Troubadour. I capitalize the term because such was an actual sect of people, and in the days before the Information Superhighway & such, their thing was to travel across the land conveying the news in storytelling songs, sometimes embellishing. The Fool of the Tarot is often shown as a jester. He entertains with song and dance, yet he is the most serious and wise of all. Nothing really means anything to him but that Kingdom that gives everything else meaning, because it is love and family. From that home full of meaning, everything that seemed meaningless is now full of meaning, as if the clouds of age and trial have parted and son, now almost father, sees the world again as if through the eyes of the child. He is about to go dancing and laughing in the rain as he descends the hill, and so will his little dog.

Looking at the image, it is raining around the castle, though not upon the hill. The fool has freedom. The castle and the heart represent not only his goal of a home, but the home from which he born. It is owned by his father. The sun is peaking out from behind the clouds, just as the son is peaking out at the castle from beside the clouds. The dog halts in awe of the prospect of home. Anxiously her tongue hangs out and she shakes excited. The fool is both smiling and crying. But the tears are for relief as much as they are for longing; for he can see from his vantage point that he is almost home (alas, it is still there! The walls are crumbling, but they have withstood many wars and now withstand much rain, and there is shelter and love inside...it is still there, and he is almost there!), just down the mountain and across the river.

The "fool"? not such a derogatory thing at all. The fool finds humor--a sign of intelligence--in life in just how graciously beautiful the ways of the world it has of balancing sunlight & rain, both essential for growth (just as innocence & experience, or thinking and acting, wrong and right, progressive & conservative).

"If the fool would persist in his folly, he would become wise."
-William Blake

A William Blake (who interpreted God to be the Poetic Genuis inherent in man) proverb that I keep coming back to is "If the fool would persist in his folly, he would become wise." In other words, go to it with your bad self...take that initiative...write your own adventure...find what you want and set your sights and actions & spirits to manifesting that goal, believing it into existence. hoping faith makes fate. what might seem crazy at first and to much of the rest of the world, should he not give up his faith in it, believing it into existence, the foolishness becomes ultimate dignity, and the dream becomes reality. Thus is the creative poet like a god. ("Do what thou wilt shall be the whole of the Law... Love is the Law...Love under will."). To be Something, all it's going to take is Initiative. The Love is There. He knows best that the best he can do is do his best. If he gives it all he's got and fails, at least he gave it all he got and he has still come that far. And there is no failure anyway, for where time does not exist (the aether) (which is the space between him & home, the heart), he is already home. If he doesn't try, he will fail anyway, and if he could've succeeded had he given it his best, and fails because he didn't, then he would be foolish, whereas in committing to take the challenge, he is the Fool...all possibilities ahead (zero), and a simple home (1) the real goal. A familiar home, longlost, now found to be not so far away. And the bridge looks to him like surely something he and his little dog can certainly handle. All that he's seen across the vast world in his traveling, when all the while all he wants is there at home. And this is the first card, the beginning of the deck, and not the last, though actually, being zero, it has no technical chronological placement; it is the citadel backbone origin which exists in everything...it's position in the deck is in eternity, as is the Fool's perspective as he travels in a zero circle...the aether just before manifestation, the thought behind the first Word.

Indeed the essence of this card lies between and within every card, for it reflects the very one who is addressing the Oracle; the limelight protagonist looking in looking out at the cards, interpreting into and from the reading. The book in his hands--the Book of Life, the Book of Love-- is both to write in and to read from at once.

The Fool is Fallen Man, having eaten of the Fruit of Knowledge of Good and Evil, seeking return to Eden, having strayed. The Prodigal Son. From clues he's collected out in the world, he believes he has the answer to the riddle posed by the evertwisting cherub with the flaming swords who guards the Tree of Life in Eden. He will come knocking, with three raps.

Beneath his book of poems he covers his heart, which peaks out at the one that looks back at it from the castle.

The Fool is Fallen Man, having eaten of the Fruit of Knowledge of Good and Evil, seeking return to Eden, having strayed. The Prodigal Son. From clues he's collected out in the world, he believes he has the answer to the riddle posed by the evertwisting cherub with the flaming swords who guards the Tree of Life in Eden. He will come knocking, with three raps.

The key number of the Fool card is 11. The pillars of the temple at the entrance to the Sanctum Sanctorum, or Holy of Holies. 11 which is 2. 74 & 56. It is ruled by air, or aether, and in this interpretation of the card, we see all aspects of it through cycle: clouds, rain, river, healthy grass, and the clear air atop the mountain. And believe me, the air is not always clear up there. It is almost humbling to see the almighty castle being pet by rain. Yet atop the hill, the prince turned fool turned wiseman, is overwhelmingly humbled so by the castle like nothing he's even cared so much about before. In his little shoulder sack he keeps his birthright. He has only to take it out his sack, show it to the doorman, and the drawbridge would be drawn, as would the doorman, a suddenly humbled servant kissing the prince's feet. The doorman exclaims his name and surprise and raises his hands to God in gratitude. His father and mother shower their returned son with gifts, who has had his play and is ready to begin the Great Work. He has both the strongest and the most loving support he could ask for. There is a warm fire and healing ailments inside the castle...family and love. He has been off on adventure and they all want to hear his stories at the dinner table (which is immense!), but for him, the real adventure has just begun.

The Fool is still the zero card, the Entered Apprentice, the young prince who is also a jester. He is a candidate who will be Raised a Master Mason the easy way, and so wants to prove up the hard way. In mathematics, sometimes he shows his work, sometimes he doesn't.

He is the source of elements, being spirit aether, the zero substance out of which all is formed...the rough ashlar....the stone which the builder refused yet becomes the headcorner stone of the entire temple. Next stage, he will be the builder himself, the initiate, Magician, the Son come to claim his Fatherly inheritance, just as Space opens up to manifest Substance. As such, it must be remembered that he is young...an open slate...a candidate for initiation, and wearing the rags of such, with one knee exposed of the intuitive left foot ready to take the first initiatory step forward, wearing the blindfold of teary eyes and flushed cheeks, all that keeps him from seeing the Light clearly...Yet. Zero is not so much the lack of quantity, but the potential of all qualities. He has only to open the book, in his hand, and the adventure begins...both reading & writing... and when he takes up the pen to write, he becomes the Magician.

He is the source of elements, being spirit aether, the zero substance out of which all is formed...the rough ashlar....the stone which the builder refused yet becomes the headcorner stone of the entire temple.

He is walking toward the other trumps of the deck, about to pass through the various cards, spiritually hoodwinked and a bound neophyte, but brave, curious, and open-minded, immersing himself upon the passage through the gates of Divine Wisdom on the path to from All-Potentiality to All-Fulfilled.

His equivalent in the playing card deck (which is modeled after the Tarot) is the joker. The wild card. Though it appears to have no value, and the figure to be young & both farcical & destitute, he hides subtly within him the resources to take on any value, even the Ace, as most required, and it is because of his simple conservativeness that he is able to do so.

The Zero card is Ain Soph, the First Cause.

A traditional interpretation of the Fool card: The beginning of a new life-cycle and all new beginnings. Energy, optimism, happiness, and force. Circumstances and occurrences that are unexpected and unplanned, and which overturn existing states. Important decisions and choices to be made.

The Turtle Tarot deck created by Tommy Baas is available for purchase. E-mail gnostictom420@yahoo.com

The Apple-Tree

Art and Knowledge of the Craft

Summer 2010

VOLUME I: ISSUE 2

In 1717 a governing authority known as the "Grand Lodge of England" was established at a meeting of four surviving lodges in the Apple Tree Tavern in London. Two Protestant clergymen, Dr. John Theophilus Desaguliers and Dr. James Anderson, were instrumental in setting up the self-styled governing body. Not all lodges were willing to submit to the rule of the new Grand Lodge, but by 1725 the original four lodges had grown to sixty four, of which fifty were in London. The Craft captured the fancy of certain members of the English aristocracy after 1721, and they in turn were flattered by the brethren. The first royal Grand Master took office in that year, and this position has since then been reserved to a nobleman.

-*Christianity and American Freemasonry*, William J. Whalen

The Apple-Tree
Art and Knowledge of the Craft

SUMMER 2010   Volume I: Issue 2

Edited by Brother Tommy Baas, cover art by Brother Tom Curtis
Freemasons Lodge #363, Milwaukee, WI

Art, essays, poetry, photography, etc., always welcome. Please submit all contributions to gnostictom@yahoo.com

"Don't tell me there are no designs on the Trestleboard..."

The Light of Morn

On a mirror-like lake in Wisconsin,
A loon calls its plaintive loon-song,
Is it music of souls lost to heaven,
Or the cry of eternity long?

The sky goes from green to deep yellow
There, 'cross the water's a fawn,
The trees are a tiara of blackness,
In the moment of earliest dawn.

Can I capture this moment ephemeral,
With brushes and paints and a can,
Or with digital camera and tripod,
Or call upon some other plan?

No, Never can it be thus captured,
In full, neither water nor sod,
It's a blessing from Heaven revealed
A sacrament 'twixt us and God.

The Architect builds and delivers,

Riches, unnumbered, untold,
To all who have eyes to perceive them,
His love, more lustrous than gold.

On a mirror-like lake in Wisconsin,
Comes a message so certain, so strong:
The Architect's there every morning,
In the sky and the water and song.

   -Brother Tom Curtis, WM

Photography by Brother Michael G. Becker

Mirrors

To look into a mirror,
  can be scary.
One will see the true self,
  aged and worn.
Look past what we see,
  find the beauty others see.
Why do we see their beauty,
  but fail to see our own?

See what I see...for I see a divine being who is loved.

Look into thy mirror,
  see the magnificence.
Look into thy mirror,
  see the beautiful creation.
The person staring back,
  can either be friend or fo...the choice is ours.
The person staring back,
  can create heaven on earth.
Or, the opposing,
  if that is what they choose.

See what I see...for I see a divine being who is loved.

-Brother Joe Lieungh

Photography by
Brother Michael G. Becker

Mushroom Sunday

Sunday afternoon in June
everybody's roller-blading around the Park
frisbees flying through the air
cutting the breeze that rolls in off the lake
down by the docks a seagull picnic flocks
the sunlight's shadow casting splits
your complexion
into two opposing
forces
the energy you reap from the angels fast asleep
on the brow of
Sunday strung out sunspots
drives you to walk further through the Mystery
of fluttering butterfly dances
above burning bush deities in waiting
spears of grass all swaying
intricate in patterns
always moving
shattered synapses
reconnecting readjusting
identity spring-cleaning
surface ripple splitting
splashes as the seagulls
dive down for Body of Christ breadcrumb
eucheristic revelation
& the mallards set up picnic beneath the drooping weeping willow
that shades the pond like a shaggy dog
& the statue of our city founder stands stoic in his unkept
garden guarding over our curious
children as kite ripples suspend familiar
colors in impermanent motion
& the poets only wish they could capture it all

fluffs of dead white

artwork by Brother Tommy Baas

dandelion powder windblown
strewn across a freshly mown
green, green grass intricate
in Shadows line the City
Sidewalk in the Sunshine
strangers in the Underpass bubbling brook
in the distance babbling carried by the Breeze
that swirls in off the Lake in Summer
solstice weekend weeperwillow waves all weaving
topsoil for the painted turtle
transit tripping transcend
leaks through leaves a-twirling
tadpole tales mosquito eggs
underneath the rocks the potato bugs
harvesting the topsoil
while anthills graze the landscape
like pyramids in Egypt
& an erupting spout of sun-speckled
spring water from the fountain sprinkling the
bathing mallards at work
& the children don't even realize they
are mortal
as buggies filled with dozing babes
in pink blankets for the Goddess
glazed in Fourth of July fireworks
across
the cloud-free sky over the Pond
which
beneath a cement bridge ponders
lifetimes older than its
patrons & blondes in their bikinis
baking in the boldness of a bewildered
Sunday setting sacrificial sunset you
don't have to dress up & go to mass to see the Masterpiece of our Christ's madness
splattered on the canvas of a day
the atmosphere intoxicating sprawled

artwork by Brother Tommy Baas

out

on a mountain top for all the heavens to see

me stealing solace from the sunshine on such a

soothing Sunday afternoon in June

on the Lily Pad

in the Cattail Territory

swans across the surface where sailors have cast their stories in webs

of wondrous wake of wading sailboat motor misguided making permanent

markings on the reality lived out

    by the mermaids of our daydream's design

    made up of fragments of our memories fractured

    by the Soul's identity in relationship

    to Infinity in the

    Grand Scheme of Serendipity

which always succumbs to something more

surreal in the poetry written by the position of our brain synapses teasing us

into tantrums brought on by silly-sigh-been spells in idle affirmation of the senses at play in the fields of daisies

& the Wind smells like everything you've ever known & loved in this lifetime

    -Brother Tommy Anthony Baas

Photography by Brother Michael G. Becker

Master of Tea Ceremonies

It is amazing to watch the master of tea ceremonies,
   Who has practiced all his life.
He has mastered his techniques,
   With precision and care.
He enjoys pouring tea,
   For others to endure.
As the water boils and whistles a tune,
   It signals the time when the master tends to his tea.

He carefully pours the boiling water,
   Over the tea and herbs.
Steeping to peak perfection,
   Is his number one task.
Allowing enough time,
   For the proper taste to delight.
It is time to serve his guests,
   One saucer at a time.

A young man approaches the Master of Tea Ceremonies,
   And offers a new way.
The master grunts and groans,
   And requests he leave him alone.
He is not interested in making tea faster or better,
   Merely perfecting his ways is all he may.
More tea does not interest him,
   Neither bigger cups.
For he has perfected his ways,
   All his life.

Do not take it personal,
   Do not dismay.
For the master of the tea ceremony,
   Is set in his ways.

You can try to change him and the way he serves,
  Ultimately it is he who has to agree to change.
You can show him the tea set,
  But it is he who has to agree.
To change the ceremony,
  To change his ways.

    -Brother Joe Lieungh

Artwork by Brother Tommy Baas

Humble

We wait for sun
We watch the moon
We cast fires
For those long gone
Our hearts remember them
Our tears water flowers
Flowers need this
We need this
It keeps us humble
Passing through thicket and forest
The presence of light remains to remind us
all is not lost
The presence of light is near again
Move with the knowledge every breath
and every vision is a blessed one

-Brother David J. White

photography by Brother Tommy Baas

The Word

by Brother Tommy Baas

A word is dead,
When it is said,
Some say.
I say it just
Begins to live
That day.

      -Emily Dickinson

In the Beginning was the Word...

    Freemasonry has been commonly described as "a peculiar system of morality veiled in allegory and illustrated by symbols." Through gathering at the same altar with men of all cultures and religious philosophies, we learn that, like a picture paints a thousand words, every symbol is at once pregnant with infinite levels of interpretation. The very structure of the Masonic ritual reveals subliminally a great truth, too oft forgotten in this divisive world beyond the Garden: that no interpretation of anything symbolized for reflection is more or less inherently accurate than another; each is only significant according to an individual's agenda for "accuracy." Since the genesis of civilization, man has used symbols to create "order out of chaos" in an indirect attempt to interpret meaning from one mind to another via otherwise arbitrary, exterior symbols. In the process of Communication some ideas are lost, some are gained, and many are nurtured. Something like what William S. Burroughs called a "third mind" is born in that womb between thought/expression, and reception/interpretation. If you could somehow communicate with this "third mind" (say through prayer, for example), or at least study it, you could learn a lot about yourself and how and why you think the way you do. In so doing you would consequently learn much about the world and how and why it works the way it does.

    The earliest mystics found that the laws of Nature seem to work isomorphically on every level of reality. They studied both the celestial bodies above and the living plants of the Earth below for patterns in God's plan, so to better understand how the same forces of Nature affect Mankind. This concept of natural cosmic isomorphism is indoctrinated in the Hermetic phrase, "as above, so below." Poets and scientists alike have noticed how well it seems to hold up, from the giant celestial bodies all the way down to the atomic level.

    This concept is one of the many levels of meaning symbolized by the Cross, the Masonic Square and Compasses, and the Star of David (with its two overlapping triangles, one grounded on the Earth and pointing up toward Heaven, the other vice versa). The Star of Solomon (son of David) and the symbol used by the esoteric French Masonic Order of Martinism are both relatively the same as the Star of David, but with lines overlapping each other, something like how the Square and Compasses overlap each other variously on each side upon the altar through the first two degrees of symbolic Masonry.

    The points of the Square and Compasses have a similar shape and meaning to the said sacred stars. Inside the broken star formed by the juxtaposition of the Square and Compasses hovers the letter

"G." This placement insinuates that it is between this geometric dichotomy—between Heaven (an idea) and Earth (its expression)—that God resides and acts. Consider that the Compass would draw a circle (representing infinity) and the Square (representing conformity) would box it in. This is what alchemists refer to as "squaring the circle." It reflects the idea of creating "order out of chaos." This is the ongoing goal in the processes of Life. We do this every day, indeed every moment, as we put our otherwise intangible thoughts into communicable words and symbols.

For the social animal, it is the very essence of a symbol or a word to act as a bridge between the infinite unknown (the Chaotic) and what we can communicate to be understood within a structured, agreed upon order. The definition of the letter "G" as it is explained in the Fellow Craft obligation, seemingly generically moral, reflects this very profound idea.

The introduction to the Gospel of John tells us that "In the beginning was the Word, and the Word was with God, and the Word was God." Christ, the "son" of this "Word" (or the idea born of this symbol within our mind) is at once also called "the Word." We can also reiterate this idea in the phrase "as above, so below." This interpretation reflects the axiom in terms of the first two facets of the Trinity, which are dualistic in nature, thus: "like father, like son."

Still we are only talking allegorically. Can talk be aught else?

The Substitute Word.

There is a word, a secret word, a seemingly nonsense word, that stands out among all other seemingly nonsense secret words that a Mason learns in the blue degrees. Not only can it not be spoken among non-Masons or written out at all, but this word, which is revealed to the initiate only after he experiences the allegorical death and raising that makes him a Master Mason, is given such reverence that it can only be spoken when two Masons meet upon the Five Points of Fellowship. It can't even be spoken above a whisper, and even then only broken up into syllables (except for the purpose of instruction), the first person saying the first syllable, the other the second, and the first person, the third. This symbolical breaking up of the Master's Word is a safeguard against those uninitiated who would unlawfully seek it. The idea is that it cannot be forcefully retrieved from just one brother; the complete word can only be spoken when two brothers meet. It is a similar idea to dividing a sacred pendant into two pieces among two friends, so that only when the two are brought together can the pendant reveal its powers. There is perhaps also metaphor here for the essential necessity of friendship if one is to have a full understanding of the meaning of life. No one man alone can hope to know what it's all about; he must always be interacting with others for a better understanding.

Because of the nature of the secrecy which surrounds this word, it makes it impossible to research it, much less write an essay on it, or even discuss it among brothers, and henceforth few attempts are ever made. When a Mason is administered a secret word, he swears by a memorized oath (which itself cannot be written down but in cipher) not to so much as hint at the word in any legible or audible form whatsoever that would even give a non-Mason the slightest chance to even guess at it. The symbolic penalties described in the oath for such a breech of information are graphically violent, though they are purely symbolic.

Due to the way in which Masonic degrees evolve and change over the years, even from one Rite or jurisdiction to another, exactly what the secret Master's Word given with the Lion's Paw grip in the Third Degree is, could very well have changed at some point. In other words, it's as hard to say just how long the very word I allude to, the one I was entrusted with when I was raised, has been given as the Master's Word of the Third Degree.

In Albert Pike's *Magnum Opus* of 1857, he published the very transcriptions of the fourth through thirty-second Scottish Rite degrees of the Southern Jurisdiction, which he himself had written. Upon reading them, one thing is obvious: they in no way, shape, or form resemble the fourth through thirty-second Scottish Rite degrees of the Northern Jurisdiction which I have been exposed to since initiated in 2005. While the degrees I have witnessed, save for the Fourteenth, are primarily mere morality plays set in various times and places from Biblical times to the American Civil War, the same degrees Pike transcribes in his Great Work resemble more the first three blue degrees, where instead of costumed as characters, those performing the initiation keep to their regular stations of the lodge as wardens, tylers, deacons, and worshipful master. Also like the three blue degrees, every one (all 29!) of Pike's Scottish Rite degrees comes with its own handshake and at least one password. I mention this because the very word I was given as the Master's Word upon being raised in the third degree is spelled out as a password for one of Pike's Scottish Rite degrees (just which one, you'll excuse me if I dutifully neglect to mention). In both cases, it is considered a "substitute" word for the original Master's Word, which was lost when Master Hiram Abiff was murdered by the three ruffians who vainly sought to extract from him the secrets of Masonry. We are told that while it is impossible now to ever retrieve the original lost word, it is a Mason's duty to seek it, believing that all which was lost will someday be found. This impresses upon a Mason the idea of Immortality and Resurrection. It would seem that the original word was even wholly ineffable. In a higher degree within the Scottish Rite, we are presented with the ineffable name of God, which we are to believe is that which was substituted for when lost. Hence it would be our duty as Masons to find God, intangible though He might be. The Substitute Word then would refer to the Son of God, the Logos, or Word, referred to in the introduction to the Gospel of John. Said gospel is the only one of the four not written in Greek, but in Hebrew. Perhaps as humans, or sons of God, we are the "substitutes" for that which is otherwise ineffable, the soul or the spirit, or God our Father.

In Pike's *Book of the Words*, which offers the etymologies of Masonry's secret words, the entry for this particular word describes it as Hebraic, and states that its Masonic usage originated with the French lodges. By deciphering the word one syllable at a time, Pike comes up with a definition that would refer to the place where the murdered one was hidden. This would make much sense. After Hiram is murdered, the Fellow Craft search all over for his body, stumbling upon it only by grace of a loose acacia plant. The candidate is then raised from this rough grave in the dirt and given a proper burial on a sacred hill, apparently in a hidden spot that can only be revealed by the word whispered to the raised candidate.

The problem that Pike admits is that though each syllable apart will yield words that together seem to refer to the place where the murdered one was hidden, the full word in summation of its syllables does not actually exist in Hebrew. He goes on trying to decipher what this combination of syllables could be referring to, even proposing results that would have it refer to the divine utterance from the Father through the Virgin Mother, Wisdom. This would certainly fit with the idea of the Word (or Son) of God.

Perhaps due to the abstract way in which Pike comes upon his definition and even presents it, perhaps because of the incredible reverence with which this secret word is guarded, I was still unsatisfied with what I had (or had not) learned of it from this little study. When I was first presented with the word upon being raised, my first guess was that it was of the angelic Enochian language. This would make sense considering how the word is broken up into syllables, which is characteristic of said language. The syllables even look like Enochian syllables. It is a language supposedly come down to Mankind via higher intelligences, with certain syllable combinations imbued with magical powers. It has only ever been used in the Ancient Mystery Schools, of which Masonry is the largest modern vehicle. It is commonly used in Thelemic practices, such as those magick rites performed by the infamous Ordo Templi Orientis co-founder Aleister Crowley, also a 33rd degree Mason. In the Old Testament we learn that Enoch lived to be 365 years old, interestingly the number of days it takes the Earth to rotate around the sun. Esoteric tradition attributes him with the very founding of language, which he brought to Earth after having walked with God while still alive. He was the grandfather of Noah, who preserved the ancient teachings in the Ark which he built in order that they may survive the Deluge. Masonic authority Albert Mackey even cites the Noachites as the first early school of what would eventually come to be called the Freemasons, since they originated the idea of Immortality and the Unity of God. For these reasons Enoch is considered the grandfather of the Mysteries.

    I am still only so familiar with the Thelemic school, but in the few and small Enochian dictionaries I have come across, I have yet to find any combination of syllables even close enough to that which makes up the Master's Substitute Word, though that very well could be due to the secretive nature of the word.

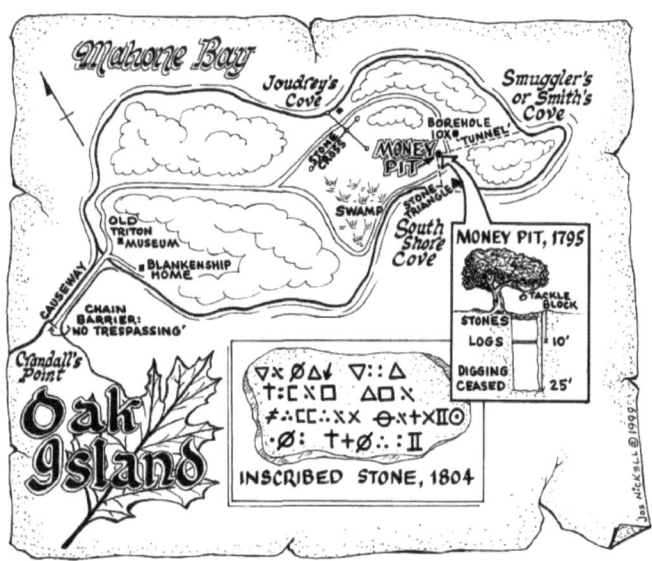

The first time I stumbled upon something that looked remotely enough like unsaid word, it was in a poorly written, yet very interesting book about the Templar treasure supposedly hidden in Nova Scotia (*The Knights Templar in the New World* by William F. Mann). If the use of this word in Masonry originated in the French lodges, and if it should refer to a place where something which was lost is now hidden, well, then I might be on to something here. The particular port in Nova Scotia where renegade French Templars fleeing persecution allegedly arrived long before Columbus has been a hot spot for legend of a buried Templar treasure since 1754. Because it is so similar to our alluded unsaid word, I will not offer the actual name of the bay in Nova Scotia where the Templars took port, but will say enough that it is a French term which refers to low-lying craft used by Pirates. It is derived from a similar term referring to a type of 16th century nautical vessel that employed both a sailing rig and oars for propulsion. This could refer to exactly the type of vessel renegade Templars would have used when fleeing France to the New World. As a matter of fact, the skull and bones symbol was originally a Masonic/Templar symbol. Hence Templar fleets were often mistaken for pirate fleets. It follows that Templar treasure can as easily be mistaken for pirate treasure. This is in fact the case in regards the treasure of Oak Island, one of the bay's many islands. Interestingly, the bay includes exactly 365 islands.

    If the common theory that modern Freemasonry was begun by, or at least was infiltrated and heavily affected by renegade Templars seeking a new organization through which to hide itself that would satisfy their religious nature yet still be open-minded enough to include those persecuted for alleged heresy, then Masonic traditions and rites could certainly have been affected by such an engagement. And if renegades wishing to remain hidden needed a secret password in order to identify their fellow men (come from all over Europe seeking sanctuary from persecution) that they might guide each other along toward the secret rendezvous point, like an underground railroad of sorts, it would stand to reason that such a secret word should allude to a secret far off meet-up place (perhaps guided by that mythological Egyptian star, which in French is *l'America*) where they could find sanctuary and even bury the prized possession that they had run off with, and begin there the New World upon that cornerstone. Legends claim this treasure could be either the Holy Grail or the Ark of the Covenant, if they are not even one and the same symbolically. Oak Island legends have it that what's buried there is a big money pit, probably pirate booty. There is reason to believe however that the buried treasure is much more than just gold.

As well as supposedly being protectors of the Grail and/or the Ark, Templar legends have them originating as the militant branch of the Priory of Sion. The Priory of course is that secret society which allegedly protects the bloodline of Jesus Christ and Mary Magdalene through the Merovingian dynasty of medieval France. The active rule of said dynasty was cut short after the Catholic church orchestrated the murder of its heir Dagobert II. Growing modern theories, with much to back them up, hold that this lost bloodline is actually what the legendary search for the Holy Grail actually alludes to.

While it is possible the Templar fleets may have carried heirs to the bloodline symbolized by the "Holy Grail"—in fact one Prince Henry St. Clair, a Templar himself, is known to have made the voyage from France to Nova Scotia—certainly one cannot literally bury a bloodline (just the outline of it on parchment), at least not like one can a treasure, nor were the Templars able to escape with much of their riches. A corpse on the other hand would certainly be something to be buried. But what dead body, even of a famous person, if not buried with gold within the coffin, would constitute such a treasure worth being carried off in a desperate flee from persecution and guarded with such secrecy?

If we think back on the original definition Pike offered of the Master's Word, or even consider at what point in the third degree allegory the word is given, it might shed some light: the murdered Master Hiram was not resurrected from the dead, he was only reburied somewhere safe, secret, and more befitting such a man. No, I am not proposing that the Templars actually had the body of the Old Testament architect in charge of building King Solomon's Temple. While there is evidence that Hiram was not a completely allegorical figure, he did not actually die in the circumstances played out in the third degree. In fact, he finished the temple and lived on for some time afterward. His personage was simply adapted into the traditional Mystery School initiatory legend. I allude instead to a much more important Biblical character, whose very flesh and bone was fashioned by angels in a virgin's womb and could certainly yield great powers. Even if not, at least the very existence of this corpse would be a threat to the orthodox suggestion that He ascended to Heaven still in the flesh. The idea that flesh could go to Heaven, though, does not only contradict the Gnostic belief that the body is an earthly tomb to be transcended, but also might seem odd in the orthodox context, considering the body is supposedly the source of all sin. Unless of course Jesus' body was different, which it certainly should be if it was fashioned by angels in Mary's womb, supposedly without even the help of Joseph's DNA (though Joseph was descended from the Davidic line according to the gospels). The Gnostics held that Jesus was not so much human at all, but like a spirit that could transcend from one body to another at whim, and actually has done so from one prophet to the next over the ages. Likely this was one way He might have escaped the crucifixion, whether from the body of Simon of Cyrene as some versions go or from an actual carpenter from Bethlehem. It was the original thought of God articulated into form, thus it was the Son of God. In the Greek, we call it the Logos. It is that which was in the beginning, was with God, and is God; it is the Word. It was a covenant from the Creator to Mankind, and may very well have been that powerful force which Moses would have been carrying in his ark, one of the many treasures credited to the Templars' possession, like the talismanic severed head of John the Baptist.

At the beginning of every blue lodge meeting, the Master's Word is whispered between the officers at the West end upon the Five Points of Fellowship and then passed across the floor by one to the East side (the source of light) of the lodge room in the same whispering protocol to be confirmed by the Worshipful Master. At the close of lodge the Word is whispered in just such a chain, but back across the East to the West end. The entire process is reminiscent of the old children's game of telephone, where the humorous object is to see just how corrupted a certain phrase can become when whispered from one to another around a circle and back to the originator of the phrase to confirm its accuracy, or if the game goes off well, its lack thereof. Could it be possible that this ritual was intended to somehow reflect such a game, thereby hinting in riddle at how the Substitute Word had been corrupted from the name of the bay in Nova Scotia as it'd been passed along? Or even, was this actually how the modern pronunciation of the Word happened to arrive in the modern ritual? Some corruption of the Word would indeed seem imminent, considering how across both time and space it was not to ever be spoken above a whisper, and only in broken up syllables, and most especially never in writing. The first time this Word was presented to me, I certainly did not hear it quite right, and may have even given it wrong to the first initiate who I had the honor of instructing.

This secret word is only ever used in initiatory instruction and the opening and closing rituals of a lodge meeting, and then only by certain officers. Never beyond that is the word and what it might mean ever discussed, nor could much research be done on it, considering even so much as typing it into a google would constitute a breech of secrecy. To the modern Freemason, the only secrets required kept are the modes of recognition, which means the handshakes and the passwords. Many of the passwords are obscure Old Testament names that anyone with even a decent knowledge of the Bible might not recognize. The words come across to the overwhelmed initiate as seemingly nonsense, nor is much of a satisfying explanation given of these words in the scripted degree instruction.

THE LION'S PAW----
ANCIENT EGYPTIAN DRAWING

Only recently did I come across the following, in regards to the Substitute Word, in the compendium *The Western Mysteries, The Key of It All, Book II* by David Allen Hulse. And finally I am not only satisfied with a theoretical definition of the Substitute Word, but I seem to have uncovered yet a new mystery concerning the Word. Apparently even the substitute we are given is secretly incomplete, perhaps to conceal it all the more, even to most Master Masons. I inserted the asterisks myself for ciphering purposes. But for educational purposes, I left spelled out the syllable variations that would be new to us.

[intro, cvii]:

The secret concerning this substitute word is its correct pronunciation. It is always written in Masonic rubrics as the three syllables M** H** B***. Yet it should be pronounced in four syllables as M** H** Boh Nay [*note: Now it seems even more to resemble a jumbling of the name of that bay in Nova Scotia... though that is still made up of but three syllables*].

...[Aleister] Crowley was aware of the fourfold nature of this secret password and lettered his own version to total his favorite number, 93 [In the Hebrew Qabalah, it would be 113].

"Modern Masonic scholarship considers the word of possible French origin [*as the name of the bay is*], because of the word B***... But the actual origin for this lost word of the third degree is Hebrew, which is the source language for so many other Masonic symbolic words. For Masonic symbolism as we know it was derived from a Renaissance magickal understanding of the Hebrew Qabalah.

As Hebrew, M** H** Boh Nay must be translated liberally; but the meaning of this lost word becomes clear in light of Hebrew, and Hebrew alone. Such a literal, liberal translation is needed in analyzing most Masonic esoteric words, for the grasp of both Hebrew and the Qabalah was not perfect in the founders of the many degrees of Freemasonry.

The correct lettering in Hebrew for M** H** Boh Nay is:

MH HBVNH = *M**? H*-Boneh?*

which literally translates as the question, "What? (MH) Is this (H) the Builder's (BVNH) (Word)?" where "Word" must be assumed. Therefore M** H** Boh Nay becomes the question "What? Is this the Builder's Word?" meaning, "Is this the real word, or the substitute word?" The answer is, of course, that M** H** B** N** is not the lost word but the substitute. The true lost word is the Tetragrammaton, the word Jehovah as the four lettered name of God in Hebrew [JHVH], the word which was written on parchment and hidden in the holy of holies of King Solomon's temple as the cornerstone.

Hulse also mentions how this word of power is found throughout much of the folklore and magickal and mystical literature of the West, and can be seen in such words as ABRACADABRA and RUMPELSTILTSKIN (don't ask me where). He goes on from the above quoted passage to describe Crowley's adoption of the substitute word in inheriting the rituals of the Ordo Templi Orientis, but that being of a non-Masonic initiatory order, I'll leave that up for the more seriously curious readers to pursue and peruse on their own. Perhaps I've said too much already.

In light of this secret within a secret—that elusive fourth syllable to the Substitute Word—it is interesting to note that the Lost Word itself has had similar variations. In his classic *Des Arte Cabalistica* (1517), the Christian mystic Johann Reuchlin (1455-1522) draws upon the *Portae Lucis*, a Latin translation of Rabbi Joseph Gikatalia's (1248-1323) *Shaarei Orah* where the concept of the Qabbalic Tree of Life first appeared in print. He believed that the Qabalah contained the doctrine of Christianity in its Western form (as opposed to the Hebrew Qabalah, derived from Abraham), and that in the age of the patriarchs before God's true name was revealed to Moses as the four-lettered Tetragrammaton, YHVH (Yod He Vauv He, in Hebrew syllables), God's true name was formerly considered the three-lettered Trigrammaton, YHV.

That would indeed fit more with the Trinity of Father, Son, and Holy Spirit. Patriachal Christianity seems to have obscured the fourth aspect of God (the second He syllable in the name), symbolically the Daughter/Bride, as categorically as they have the role of the true Beloved disciple, Mary Magdalene. Gnostic Christianity, which is all the more faithful to Christianity's mixed pagan and Jewish roots, seems to know better. The early basis of the Christian Qabbalah added yet a fifth Hebrew letter, Shin (literally, "nail"), to the name of God, creating the Pentagrammaton, YHShVH. This is also the Hebrew spelling of the name Jesus, derived from Jeshua, or Joshua.

The story we are familiar with concerning Jesus's life and death and resurrection is actually a Gnostic/Jewish adaptation of the archetypal Mystery School Legend used for the initiation of candidates, as evident by the undeniable similarities with Mystery School heroes such as Osiris, Dionysus, and Tammuz. All have their foundation in the Shamanic tradition, where the Shaman dies a symbolic "death" into the Underworld ("Hades" or "Hell" or the Lower Realm in Western terms) by means of hallucinogenic drugs, to come back out enlightened and ready to preach and heal. Note that Jesus, Moses, Joseph, and John the Baptist all first travelled through Hades or the Wilderness or some kind of bondage (also symbolically referred to as Egypt in the allegories) before beginning their ministrations. Freemasonry being the modern vehicle of the initiatory Mystery School tradition, Hiram Abiff's adapted story also yields similar symbolic concepts. This in fact, as laid out in the papal bull, is the real reason why the Catholic Church considers Freemasonry to be a blasphemy.

YHVH, a Four-Letter Word? (‡)

In the Fourteenth Degree of the Scottish Rite (commonly agreed to be the most touching and beautiful of all Masonic degrees) and the Royal Arch Degree of the York Rite, we are reminded with particular emphasis of the commandment not to take the Lord's name in vain. This is not because of any mystical ramifications in the utterance of any particular set of syllables (‡). Nor, as the initiated will tell you, do the letters G-O-D spell the true ineffable name of God any more than they spell in reverse the name on my dog's tags. Even the Tetragrammaton is but a set of symbols, its four Qabalic letters on but one level representing the four basic elements that all life is made up of. The Jews and Gnostics used many different names for God in their incantations to avoid using His unspeakable real name, which Leonard R.N. Ashley in *The Complete Book of Magick* asserts is "Emeth. (4)." But even, what the hell might that mean? It's just more letters put together to form a set of syllables. Just as a rose by any other name smells just as sweet, and a map is only a scale representation of a certain territory, so too is even the idea of "God" just a communicable representation of an invisible archetype, an ideal inherent in the Mind.

In the Qabalah, the twenty-two Hebrew letters are transmuted in various ways to create different divine names in a manner reflectively isomorphic to how the various elements are transmuted by alchemical formulas to create new substances. The Ancient Eastern Tradition focused on but three core elements—Fire, Air, and Water—while later in the Western Tradition, we consider the basic elements (the Builder's bricks of the Temple, if you Will) to be fourfold, adding Earth to the equation. I'm inclined to wonder if this "transformation" has any isomorphism with the mentioned change of God's name from a Trigrammaton to a Tetragrammaton after Moses spoke to God through that highest of all elements, Fire. Elsewhere in the Old Testament we read of God giving life to Man by blowing upon the dust (Earth) and breathing (Air) into his nostrils, and further regenerating Mankind by the Great Flood (Water). When reading that on the First Day, God created the Heavens and the Earth, and then later the Waters, we are reading a very explicit alchemical formula. In Chapter 3, Section 3 of the *Sepher Yetzirah* (one of the two original sourcebooks of the Qabalah, said to have been written by Abraham), we read how through the Three Mothers (represented by the three Supernal Sephiroth in a triangle atop the Tree of Life, isomorphic with both the Christian Trinity and the three original Master Masons at the building of Solomon's Temple, which is representative of the Universe), the entire universe was created with also the addition of the fourth element:

> The Heavens were produced from Fire
> The Earth from the Water and the Air
> from the Spirit (Breath of God or Kether)
> like a balance between the Fire and the Water

Qabalists believe that the creation of the Universe was carried out through the manipulative invocation of Hebrew letters. This may shed some light on the mysterious introduction to the Gospel of

John. Nor should it seem strange that the Bible be a compendium of alchemical formulas allegorically explaining the Creation of Man and the Universe. Through the Rosicrucians and the Arthurian Legends most notably, and also certainly through Freemasonry for those in the know, alchemical formulas have always been secretly encapsulated through seemingly absurd mysterious allegories. All these ideas are also perfectly congruent with the Mysteries of the East, particularly in Taoism, with its *I Ching* oracle based on 64 trigrams representing variously transmuted elements. Yet another code—DNA—is based on 64 codons of varying triple-nucleotide sequences, or amino acids. Verily, the mRNA coil is but the modern scientific version of the Serpent in Eden, Jacob's Ladder up to Heaven, the Winding Stairs of the FC Degree, the lightning movement through the Tree of Life, the rising of Kundalini energy through the Chakras, and the caduceus staff yielded by such figures as Moses, Hermes, Thoth, and Mercury.

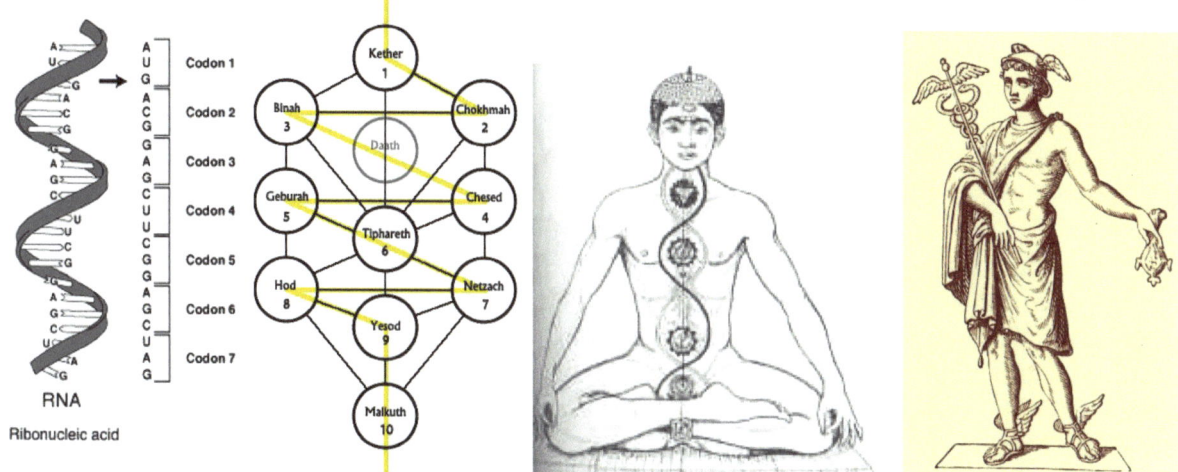

The pagans, like the Hindus, were not necessarily polytheists, but used many interchangeable names to describe different manifestations for different attributes of one all-encompassing God, similar to how Christians breakdown God into the Trinity of three different aspects of God. Both pagan and Hindu mythologies receive frequent citation in the morally philosophical digressions of Albert Pike in that most essential of Masonic masterpieces, the classic *Morals & Dogma of the Ancient & Accepted Scottish Rite*. Even mystic Christians and Qabalic Jews hailed God by a few different names, sometimes as angels or archangels, according to varied aspects of the deity in their incantations. This is in evidence even in the Bible; consider: Elijah, Yahweh, Jehovah, Adonai, Elohim, Gabriel, Michael, and Immanuel, to name a few. And as they say in Latin on the Masonically-encrypted dollar bill, *E Pluribus Unum*… "Out of many, One."

I would argue that a pagan should no sooner be denied membership in a Masonic lodge than a Hindu, Jew, or a Christian. Nor do I pretend to understand the apparent hostility toward paganism in boastingly open-minded Masonic rhetoric. Indeed it is from this very allegorical pantheism that much of our symbolism, as well as that of all major religions, is derived.

When recently objections were raised against a Hindu candidate seeking membership in a British lodge in India, the Grand Lodge concluded that the seemingly separate pantheistic gods were simply symbolic manifestations of various aspects of one Supreme Being. The candidate was then accepted into the order (*Born in Blood*, Robinson, pg. 255). Logically the same precedent should be considered for pagans.

For an establishment whose greatness is derived from the bringing together of men of all faiths with many different names and aspects encapsulating that one ineffable God of the natural, pre-lingual religion of Man (who in deliberately vague terms of our own symbolic stonemason terminology we refer to as the Supreme Architect of the Universe), this should seem not only an easy but a truly glorious concept to grasp. Indeed it should just be assumed.

Speaking of otherwise intangible concepts with infinite levels for interpretation in an allegorical and pantheistic manner, one is able to keep a much more open mind about the identity of God. In so doing one realizes that any way earthly words could describe Him/Her/It would inevitably be no more than allegorical and truly "in vain." It is for this very reason that it is considered blasphemous idolatry in Islam to depict at all an image of Mohammed. The very first line of Lao Tzu's *Tao te Ching* implies an essence that precedes all conceptualized thoughts of "God": indeed, "The Tao that can be told is not the eternal Tao."

The Creation (the "First Thought" or "son" of the Creator God by the Earthly Virgin, in Taoism, "the Mother of All Things," whose womb is the realm of all archetypes) as well as any thought or concept since, is logically pre-lingual, though manifested words may create more thoughts still. Indeed everything is just a symbol of everything else, and everything is isomorphic on varying levels of interpretation.

To assume pagans "worshipped the sun" because their main god(s) was (were) depicted by the symbol of a sun is just as absurdly short-sighted as would be to assume Christians worship the sun because they depict Jesus with a halo behind His head, and that He "dies" and "rises again" according to celestial cycles on dates significant to each corresponding solstice (another concept borrowed from the pagans, and one we use at the opening and closing of every lodge!). That solar glow behind His head would also seem to double as a lion's mane, denoting his kingship symbolically. Indeed the "sun" and "lion" share the same root word in the Egyptian etymology. This reflects a pantheistic use of animal symbols, and actually refers to the sun's movements through the zodiac of Leo. It would seem actually that pagans, much like the Taoists, actually worship and have always worshipped none other than the forces of Nature. So too do Christians, as we can see when we learn to read the symbols by more than just their outer manifestations.

The languages of early civilizations were largely made of analogous symbols abstracted into archetypes through the Creative Conscience of the leading protagonists in the evolution of Mankind at the time. People described what they saw in images that their listeners could understand. In the somewhat manipulative priestly/governmental tradition, they imbibed such in just the right manner, pregnant with just the right connotations so as to invoke a certain response and nourish a certain reality tunnel in the minds and nervous systems of the sheeply public receiving the new information. You will notice how all thought and language seems to have a psychosomatic effect, particularly among people speaking the same language. The romancer who speaks in French to the naïve, young girl knows that sometimes even using a different language will have a greater affect. This phenomenon becomes especially evident when we consider either the naivete of the spiritually vulnerable or the fanatically esoteric-minded. Whether of their own accord or at the mercy of their "masters," they are inclined to feel by the regimented focus of their understanding that certain incantations to certain strange gods are somehow that much more effective in the dead languages of famous past mystics. But Latin, Aramaic, and even Enochian are no better or worse vessels for the communication of ideas than English, German, or gibberish, so long as the desired ideas are articulated effectively and the listener accepts their imbibed meaning.

The same phenomenon is true for people of the same or a different religion. All possible sects are simply different culture-responsive languages describing the same phenomena of Nature that reflect the secrets of the soul, both being of the same Source. Often the emphasis may be on a different angle of a grand idea, but 7x7x7 still comes out the same as 7 cubed in the end. Beyond conditioned denotations and connotations, no one is more or less particularly responsive to any certain word or interpretation of a concept than your dog will only respond to the name you train her by.

What makes using God's name in vain—and of course, this would seem all the more true for people who believe in God, especially an interpretation of God conditioned in their minds according to established connotations imbibed by a certain dogmatically superstitious religion—is that when you do so, you are blaming the forces of Nature on something that goes wrong. While they may be to blame in some indifferent way, speaking of them in such a harsh manner psychosomatically manifests a counter-evolutionary feeling of despair through a physical expression of inner doubt. As I like to say, Man versus Nature will never succeed, but he will prosper only when he realizes his integral alliance within it.

Nature can't be "wrong"—indeed it knows not such an arbitrarily connotative dichotomy—thus it could only be one's chosen perception among the infinite possible that should be changed. It's never good to allow negative energy to keep rolling along collecting karmic snow and getting stronger, creating a lofty snowball of coldness. He who throws such will feel the same coldness in his own hand that the target receives.

Toss the *I Ching* on a daily basis and you'll find that happiness only comes from being patient and having faith in the ways of the world. Basically, if you stick with the Sage through the hard times, it'll carry you through to the good times. Life is a fluctuating progression of darkness and light, after all.

While your "curses" may be "just words," all words are inherently curses in that their very utterances invoke certain psychosomatic reactions, often different from person to person, but predictable enough to ascribe to a system of what's "normal behavior." By this consensus "morality," the alphas of the tribe filter a cultural agenda into concrete familiar symbols, pregnant with meaning and connotation, through which others can learn what is "the normal way to live." This may explain the popularity of "reality" TV programs.

Our unspoken thoughts are only so much less psycho- and physical-effective. You would think that you wouldn't need to use an established language just to communicate with yourself, but the fact that you do implies a barrier between our conscious mind and our grasp of the Cosmos, the stuff of which makes up our silent soul. Here is the Tragedy of the Poet, and thus is the moral of the Tower of Babel. So we describe otherwise intangible concepts and ideas, like the forces of Nature, in a language that becomes more and more arbitrary and yet narrowly understood as it evolves. In so doing we lose that free and unfiltered understanding of the very thing we seek to know. We know that the "map" is not the "territory," but as we use words to communicate, we deflate our understanding of the world as it gets tangled in our minds by the handicaps of language, so that "stella" may cause a different chemical reaction within us than "star," though they mean the same or similar; so realizes the Poet. As our understanding of the world deflates, consequently, the world itself deflates. Keep in mind, YOU are the answer to the old Zen koan, "Who is the master who makes the grass green?" Now don't curse yourself.

The Gnostic philosopher Valentinus pointed out that because human beings created the language of religious expression, humanity, in effect, created the divine world; thus the Imagination of Man, which contains All yet is inside All, "is really he who is God over all." Eastern philosophy would seem to agree with this statement. What naturally precedes all filtered and concrete articulation is what William Blake called the "Poetic Genuis." This he considered "God" to be. At the very highest, it could be considered intuition. Even in what we call "automatic writing" or "divine intervention," since its expression must take place within a human capacity, at best it could be considered a bridge between God or Carl Jung's idea of the Collective Unconscious and the mind of Man, or the Personal Unconscious. It could certainly not take place without Man. Thus the best agreement we can rationally hold with those who would call things "supernatural" is that God could not exist without Man. The very term "supernatural" assumes a self-defeating concept in itself and nothing more than a theoretical concept; even "ghosts" or "hallucinations" would have to have some footing within Nature if any Natural being existing in the Natural realm could claim to perceive or sense them on any level at all with their Natural senses. Indeed nothing could exist on any plane of reality that could not be perceived or sensed, or it would be nothing, existentially speaking. My best friend Amelia likes to point out how "supernatural" actually means just that... *extra* natural, as opposed to "unnatural," as some might assume the term means.

(‡) ... *Or is it?! Indeed, in the Western Esoteric Tradition, of which Freemasonry is the vehicle of inheritance, the correct pronunciation of certain words is believed to give the speaker power over the objects they define, similar to how speaking your pet dog's name makes him/her obedient to your commands. Thusly did Adam give names to all the creatures over which God said that man would have dominion. In other words, to know and speak the true name of God would be to have power to petition the will of God through invocative prayer! Thus why such words are kept so secret, and considered "magic words," and why an initiate's moral character must be so rigorously tried before he is entrusted with such powerful passwords, and thus the danger in using them in vain.*

The Turtle Tarot
Created by Brother Tommy Baas

1 ~ The Magician

There is an old Buddhist proverb: "Who is the magician that makes the grass green?"

Like so many things (including Freemasonry, the Illuminati, Rosicrucianism, Templarism, Gnosticism, the OTO, Crowley, Wilhelm Reich, Carl Jung, etc), I was introduced to this quote by the late writer Robert Anton Wilson. Wilson was a self proclaimed "Guerilla Ontologist," who understood and used for good the power of the Word to manipulate perception, and thus reality. As my friend Max Klapperman, who gave me my first Wilson book, put it: Wilson's little trick is that by the time you've finished reading the *Illuminatus! Trilogy*, he's managed to subliminally initiate you into the Illuminati. Indeed it is a good brainf***, and my way of thinking is that much more clear and enlightened since reading RAW's work. Max also commented, as I was reading RAW's *Masks of the Illuminati*, on how a writer is able to subliminally mold you into a certain reality tunnel as you read. Wilson's thing was more to make you more aware of this and to keep your mind open, rather than to convince you of something, as is the typical author(ative) way. He encouraged avoiding perception-controlling verbs like "is" (see Count Alfred Korzybski's E-prime language) and always maintained humility, encouraging readers to question everything, especially his own stubborn statements.

With the ideas, writing style, and thinking exercises that he offered to the reader, he broke down reality by the reflection of words and their interpreted meanings, hand-in-hand breaking down for us the way our minds work. With his best friend, legendary psychedelic guru Timothy Leary, he exposed the process of brainwashing so that we may be more aware of how commonly it happens and how to defend against it. Wilson also introduced me to pioneer semanticist Count Alfred Korzybski, who said, "Those who control our symbols, control us." The good magician knows the difference between white magick and black magick. In fact, black magick is not an independent system; it has no core symbols of its own...it is only white magick backwards. In invoking God, spelling the Tetragrammaton backwards is as bad as spelling it forwards is good. Drawing a pentagram is all good...drawing it upside-down is bad. With the assumption that most people are right-handed, black magick has been nicknamed the "left-handed" method for this reason. You've all heard the saying, "Let not the right hand know what the left hand is doing." This has nothing to do against left-handed people, who are actually all the more in tune with their creative energy, being right-brained (everything works in a balanced cross). When doing an I Ching toss, it is best to shake the coins with your left hand. If you draw a pentagram with your left hand, as long as it isn't upside-down, you're all good; perhaps even more so because you create a cross-balance in act and expression. I know a left-handed poet who can take both the dark and light of life and by expression make it Pure and Beautiful and Good. By this I mean by way of expression she actually alters the mood of reality, churning dark into light. And mood directly affects reality, because it affects both our actions and how others react. The Good Magician is consciously aware of these factors.

    The Magician's magic wand here is a pen (and if you'll look closely, you'll see it is purple, a royally sacred color). It could also be a paintbrush. While his right hand writes, his left hand holds to a passage he is reading. Constantly both learning and teaching is the dedicated Magician. By the light of the outside world shining through his study room's window from behind and by the self-lit light of a singular candle, the magician writes worlds into existence from his pregnant mind. In Freemasonry, three candles on the altar are called the Lesser Lights, and the Bible, Square, & Compasses are called the Greater Lights. The two mason's tools which make our fraternity's star are seen here on the poet's desk (his altar). Initially one is told that the compass symbolizes being well-rounded and that the square means to keep one's actions on the square. More esoterically, the compass draws infinity, a perfect cycle, and the square boxes the circle into an organized perception. By these two complementing ways does man perceive from the inside out. Indeed there is so much more within the vault of one's mind than there is in the "vast" world outside the windows of our eyes.

    The job of the Magician is to recreate that world going on inside his Imagination and to manifest it into reality. To make Heaven on Earth. Hence, it is the will of the Imagination that makes the grass to be green. As taught in Buddhism, "reality" is an agreed upon illusion manifested by the mind perceiving it. But, you say, then how come I can't change it just as easily? Simply drawing the grass blue on a piece of paper only makes the grass on that paper blue. Bob Wilson also said, "Reality is what you can get away with." One thing we need to keep in mind is that we are everywhere surrounded by a million magicians just like us, and that Truth is an agreement. Reality is created from the constant interplay between both our personal will and the will of the rest of the world. This interaction determines Fate. Oracles can hint potential futures according to the forecast of pending circumstances, as in agreement with the student's current mental disposition, his/her attitude, and will. The affective Magician must be clearly aware of circumstances, which are often the combined byproducts of the will of other Magicians, each with their own circumstances and agendas. The good Magician constantly draws upon oracles with quiet respect, which by synchronistically drawn symbols reflect the relationship of the mood of the hand which shuffles and draws the cards and that of the archetypes whose spirits reveal in symbols, the principle of As Above, So Below. By revealing a seemingly "random" (by the proverbial element of "chance," which is simply the present patterns of Fate which we're blinded from understanding by its contention with the present patterns of our Will) of mythically symbolized archetypes (too abstract to be understood any other way better, though very, very real), Oracles help us to be the more aware of how our personal Will is presently affecting and affected by Fate, helping us know all the better how to act accordingly with what we can expect of present circumstances. As the Grateful Dead sing, "I can tell your future, just look what's in your hand."

    By being aware, we know all the better how best to go about using our will. When we align our Will with Fate, everything false into place as it should. This is the Way taught in Taoism. Contemplate what Lao Tzu meant by "Do by non-doing and all will be done" and what Aleister Crowley meant by "Do what thou wilt shall be the whole of the Law. Love is the Law. Love under Will." These mantras mean neither necessarily to just go with the flow nor just to do whatever you want and that will be right. It means if you are truly acting in tune with your conscious will, you will succeed seemingly effortlessly, because the Will, being a child of Fate, is magnetically in tune with Fate. When mind over matter doesn't work, the relationship between mind and matter is blocked by misunderstanding of either circumstances or feelings or both.   There is an element of hedonism in this philosophy, but only insofar as what feels good is good when your conscience is healthy and aware, i.e., in tune with the Collective Conscience. At this point, one is all happy and all powerful, glowing with life, capable of everything because completely aware of and in tune with the ways of his/her natural environment. A good Magician is constantly studying everything and keeps his/her bag of tools everywhere he/she goes, like a turtle shell.

    The Magician here looks like a young monk, and that is how he lives; in solitude and in love with something sacred to him. The grail in the picture here is both for nourishment and intoxication, either/or, according to either the needs or whims of the partaker's spirit. The bird in the wind is both observing and singing, in between worlds of outside and in. The rose on the cross is the blossoming soul out from the four elements, which the Magician is crucified to, as the soul within the body. In learning from and interacting with them, he/she understands his own nature that much more, being of the same stuff. And the soil, sun, air, and wind become the fertile means of his/her soul's resurrecting bloom, rather than the means by which he/she is buried.

    A personal mantra of mine is: Don't ask questions when you can all the more affectively take actions/attitudes to manifest the answer you want. The FREEmason seeks out membership of his own initiative and Freewill; it cannot be solicited. By this assertive act he reflects the Creative who makes the world. The shape of the number 1 reflects the masculine phallus, the wand/pen, the first line drawn. The Magician (1) is the Fool (0) having been initiated into the Mystery, un-hoodwinked and shown Light, armed with knowledge and the wand of his pen, ready to begin the Path through the rest of the Deck.

    Crowley, who in the Thoth deck refers to this card as the Juggler, describes it as "the adult form of the first emanation, the Fool," but also as "the Son, the manifestation in act of the idea of the Father." Indeed in the cycle of life, the Son born of the Father becomes, through maturation, the Father himself. The Magician is the Son of God as interpreted in Christianity as interchangeable with God. The Magician understands what Jesus meant that He did nothing except by the Father working through Him. The Magician derives his magic as a natural vehicle born of God's Grace.

    "In the beginning was the Word, and the Word was with God, and the word was God. The same was in the beginning with God. All things were made by him; and without him was nothing made. In him was life; and the life was the light of men. And the light shineth in the darkness; and the darkness comprehendeth not."
-introduction to The Gospel of John

    Indeed to those unenlightened in the darkness of atheism, magick appears unreal and the world a random meaningless mystery, whereas those in the Light know magick to be very real, and so being in Light, understand the ways of the world homeopathically as one within it, and are thus able to affect it by will.

The Turtle Tarot deck created by Tommy Baas is available for purchase. E-mail
gnostictom420@yahoo.com

Photos of the Alamo

taken by Brother Brian Jahns

A.D. 1848. A.D. 1948

The Birthplace of Freemasonry in West Texas

This plaque was dedicated January 15, 1948 by Alamo Lodge No. 44, A.F. & M., commemorating the one hundredth anniversary of the chartering of the lodge and honoring those pioneer Masons of that era who founded the lodge upon this site.

A.L. 5848. A.L. 5948.

HONORING THESE MASONS: James Bonham, James Bowie, **David Crockett**, Almaron Dickenson, William Barret Travis, and those unidentified Masons who gave their lives in the Battle of the Alamo, March 6, 1836. Erected by the Grand Lodge of Texas A.F.&M. March 6, 1976.

Contributed brother Jeff Farkas, jfarkas@americanconservators.com

"THE SURENDER OF GRANADA"
Oil/Canvas, signed and dated 1917 LL, "35 X 47" Inches, Condition excellent, Original frame, Price to you: $10,000.00

THE SURRENDER OF GRANADA

From Wikipedia, the free encyclopedia

Muhammad XI, d. 1538, last sultan of Granada in Spain (1482–92); also called Boabdil by the Spanish. He seized the throne from his father and thus plunged Granada into civil war at the time the Castilians were beginning their attack on the kingdom. As the Christians overran western Granada, Muhammad secretly promised (1487) them that he would surrender the city of Granada in return for some cities held by the rival Granadian party. However, he repudiated the agreement, and in Apr., 1491, the Castilians laid siege to Granada. After valiant resistance, Muhammad surrendered in Jan., 1492, and fled to Morocco. His surrender marked the end of Moorish rule in Spain, and he is the subject of a number of romantic legends.

Boabdil (a corruption of the name Abu Abdullah, or, in full, Abu 'abd Allah Muhammad XII, Arabic:
) (1460?–1527) was the last Moorish king of Granada (of the Nasrid dynasty). He was also called *el chico*, the little, and also *el zogoybi*, the unfortunate. A son of Muley Abul Hassan, king of the *taifa* of Granada, he was proclaimed king in 1482 in place of his father, who was driven from the land.

Boabdil soon after sought to gain prestige by invading Castile. He was taken prisoner at Lucena in 1483, and only obtained his freedom by consenting to hold Granada as a tributary kingdom under Ferdinand and Isabella, king and queen of Castile and Aragon. The next few years were consumed in struggles with his father and his uncle Abdullah ez Zagal.

In 1489 Boabdil was summoned by Ferdinand and Isabella to surrender the city of Granada, and on his refusal it was besieged by the Castilians. Eventually, on 2 January, 1492, Granada was surrendered. In most sumptuous attire the royal procession moved from Santa Fe to a place a little more than a mile from Granada, where Ferdinand took up his position by the banks of the Genil. A private letter written by an eyewitness to the bishop of Leon only six days after the event preserves the scene. With the royal banners and the cross of Christ plainly visible on the red walls of the Alhambra: ...the Moorish king with about eighty or a hundred on horseback very well dressed went forth to kiss the hand of their Highnesses. Whom they received with much love and courtesy and there they handed over to him his son, who had been a hostage from the time of his capture, and as they stood there, there came about four hundred captives, of this who were in the enclosure, with the cross and a solemn procession singing the Te Deum Laudamus, and their highnesses dismounted to adore the Cross to the accompaniment of the tears and reverential devotion of the crowd, not least of the Cardinal and Master of Santiago and the Duke of Cadiz and all the other grandees and gentlemen and people who stood there, and there was no one who did not weep abundantly with pleasure giving thanks to Our Lord for what they saw, for they could not keep back the tears; and the Moorish King and the Moors who were with him for their part could not disguise the sadness and pain they felt for the joy of the Christians, and certainly with much reason on account of their loss, for Granada is the most distinguished and chief thing in the world...

Christopher Columbus himself refers to the surrender on the first page of his Diario de las Derrotas y Caminos: After your Highnesses ended the war of the Moors who reigned in Europe, and finished the war of the great city of Granada, where this present year [1492] on the 2nd January I saw the royal banners of Your Highnesses planted by force of arms on the towers of the Alhambra, which is the fortress of the said city, I saw the Moorish king issue from the gates of the said city, and kiss the royal hands of Your Highnesses...

Exile

Legend has it that as the royal party moved south toward exile, they reached a rocky eminence which gave a last view of the delectable city. Boabdil reined in his horse and surveying for the last time the Alhambra and the green valley that spread below he burst into tears. "You do well," said his unsympathetic mother, "to weep like a woman for what you could not defend like a man." The spot from which Boabdil looked for the last time on Granada is still shown, and is known as "the last sigh of the Moor" (*el último suspiro del Moro*).

The vanquished Nasrid was given an estate in Alpujarras, a mountainous area between the Sierra Nevada and the Mediterranean Sea, but he soon crossed the Strait of Gibraltar to Fez, where he died in 1533.

THE PAINTER

With all the historical information Elizabeth Frida Fichtner began to compose a great painting. Elizabeth was born in Baden, Germany, in 1876. She came to America in 1895. Elizabeth was a great painter and she did many commissions and portraits, air brush painting and conservation work, for Bresler Art Gallery in Milwaukee. She returned to Munich, Germany to study art at the famous ALTE PINAKOTHEK Art School from 1909-1912. On her return to the United States she attended classes at the Chicago Art Institute and Milwaukee Art Schools where she received the same instruction as in Munich. Their instructor was the well known AMERICAN artist CARL MAAR. Frida was proud to be an AMERICAN PAINTER she received many awards. Elisabeth Fichtner died in 1945. There are150 works all in private hands none of her works ever reached any auction houses.

In 1717 a governing authority known as the "Grand Lodge of England" was established at a meeting of four surviving lodges in the Apple Tree Tavern in London. Two Protestant clergymen, Dr. John Theophilus Desaguliers and Dr. James Anderson, were instrumental in setting up the self-styled governing body. Not all lodges were willing to submit to the rule of the new Grand Lodge, but by 1725 the original four lodges had grown to sixty four, of which fifty were in London. The Craft captured the fancy of certain members of the English aristocracy after 1721, and they in turn were flattered by the brethren. The first royal Grand Master took office in that year, and this position has since then been reserved to a nobleman.

-*Christianity and American Freemasonry*, William J. Whalen

The Apple-Tree
Art and Knowledge of the Craft

AUTUMN 2010   Volume I: Issue 3

Edited and cover art by Brother Tommy Baas
Freemasons Lodge #363, Milwaukee, WI

Art, essays, poetry, photography, etc., always welcome. Please submit all contributions to gnostictom@yahoo.com

"Don't tell me there are no designs on the Trestleboard..."

Autumnal Gold

It's the smell in the air that enriches
It's the smell of the earth and the sky
It's the crispness of cool in the sunshine
It's the gold of the leaves sailing by

It's the time of the short breath of daylight
When the Equinox comes and then goes
It's the music of geese heading Southward
To a land far away from the rose

The squirrels are all busy at Noontime
Preparing for that which must come
The black walnut shells are not broken
The pumpkins, the color of rum

The corn in the fields stands ripened
light brown in the rustle of Fall
The rawk of the crows overhead now
Then off to the trees near the wall.

The maples are red with a splendor
With color from the Architect's brush
The trunks and the branches, imperial
Vibrating with the tune of the thrush.

It's the smell in the air that enriches
It's the smell of the earth and the sky
It's the beauty of Autumn primeval
It's the gold of eternity's high.

       -Tom Curtis

One with you...

I am one with you,
you are one with me.
I smile and you smile back.
I grimace and you grimace back.
I look up to the heavens,
 they shine down on me.

My eyes shut and I see no longer;
a new world begins.
I hear voices all around me,
mostly my own thoughts.
Why have I not seen so clearly before?

I failed to see the darkness...

I thank you...for my friends.
...for the words they speak.
...for the seekers who find truth.
...for allowing me to see myself as my brother.
...for doing unto them as they would do unto me.

      -Joe Lieungh

Ready for Battle

It is I who looks from above, down at the darkened sea.
I am saddened by the fish that have died; sharks that have preyed on innocent crustaceans.
With spear in hand and head held high, I prepare for battle.
It is not my strength or my wit that hath struck them down, but words of wisdom casting out the nets.
I seek further knowledge of truth that lies within.
I know it exists, I merely have forgotten.
I have known this truth for all my soul, but when born to flesh haste I forgot.
Open my Eyes.
Open my Ears.
Mainly open, my Heart to all the souls.

      -Joe Lieungh

Suburban Farm

open the country highway
up the gravel driveway to the rustic farmhouse
where barking dogs come out to greet
the slowing engine of the station wagon
cats scatter beneath porch steps
& gleaming in the doorway the angel of autumn
in an old embroidered smock for catching pumpkin guts
there's cider on the stove
there's microbrews in the cooler
there's candy corn in the bowls out on the counter
the pumpkin patch stretches out along the roadside
where haystack witches, bed sheet ghosts,
& cardboard skeletons will welcome trick-or-treaters
with mock displays of ceremonial horror
 walking back through crackling leaves
the roundest, heaviest, most fitting for a face, plump pumpkin carried
before my belly like I was due with child at any instant
plop it down on newspapers for the initial stab
& we are ready for the lobotomy of pumpkin brains
one bucket for shake & one for seeds
sister's ready to put another tray in the oven

I dare you to find a reason why life sucks!

trace the eyes trace the nose trace the teeth & carve
out the face of autumn through which candlelight will shine
gargoyle heads for front porch steps
our ritual is ready
now off with me on a short hayride
to smell the brisk air
& mellow your senses as
helicopter leaves fall from a trellis of tall trees
crumpled up & tangled in your hair which changes color
in the sunlight like leaves as down the path
blackbirds caw against the silence
insisting that it is not fall, but autumn

      -Tommy Baas

Grandpa's Apple Cider

in the low autumn sunlight
across reds, oranges, yellows
front yard orchard
picking up the least bruised of the
half-ripe apples of the harvest
hardened amongst yellowed grass patches
piles of discard shoveled up for the
wheelbarrow ride out to the compost
we bartering with the yellow jackets for the better bites
bucket after bucket brought back
for washing, swashing, slushing out the bubbly juices
pool of brown bath for struggling bumblebees
whose last breath will be of our brisk cider
before it is boiled out for salmonella
& bottled up for refrigerators
& served up for relatives for the long, cold holiday season
in River Hills, Wisconsin

    -Tommy Baas

Black Above Blue

The black above the blue
Where the atmosphere
kisses space
Peace is found in the ever expanding
forever
Where every moment that has ever been
happens again and again
Like cosmic tides
and solar waves
The endless desire for darkness to reverse
and turn itself inside out

    -David White

Genetic Conference

Burn away dust and rock
Stars and comets shed their bodies
and become new boys and girls
falling to Earth
and as they arrive here mothers and fathers
wrap them in warm blankets
and pray for their happiness

    -David White

Use Your Words

Tutor's Story
by Tommy Baas

I may be one of the few in the field who was not personally inspired into it due to having a child or a loved one diagnosed with a reading disability, or having struggled with one myself. Having been born with great eyesight, a knack for deciphering symbols, and a lust for language, it became my duty in life to assist those less fortunate in those respects. My calling came primarily through a lifelong passion for the language, both in reading and writing, poetry and prose, and specifically from a creative standpoint.

I was a quiet, introspective kid growing up. To this day, as my girlfriends can attest, I do my best communicating when I have the time and space of the Written Word on my side. In 7th Grade at Webster Middle School in Cedarburg, Wisconsin, I broke a school record, which I'm sure still stands as strong as Hank Aaron's home run record, for filling up 8 notebooks of free journal writing. These diaries got me through the hardest parts of puberty and would prove the founding record of my niche in life as a writer. The Written Word not only saved my life psychologically and emotionally in adolescence, but also established for myself who I was and what my path would be in Life. But one does not have to be a "Writer" for the Written Word to have a profound effect on anybody; it works with all avenues where clear communication is key, i.e., everywhere.

My 6th and 7th grade English teacher, Mr. Ross, rewarded me for my prolificness with not only a rarely granted A+ for the class, but also with souvenirs signed by two of my favorite writing subjects and boyhood heroes: a blue notebook signed by the Milwaukee Brewers' Paul Molitor and a picture signed by Led Zeppelin's Robert Plant. Both signatures encouraged me to "keep on writing!" And so keep on I did. In college, one of my English professors turned out to be the wife of Mr. Ross. She too gave me special recognition for my prolificness, though she wished I'd vary my subject matter a little more. Part of why I stayed in college so long was because I was having a little too much fun. After about eight years of learning more at coffeeshops and in my bedroom than I ever did going to classes, I finally earned a Bachelors in English with a focus in Creative Writing from the University of Wisconsin-Milwaukee in 2003.

My secondary inclinations toward the field came through (a) my experience working with youth and (b) as a young 32nd Degree Scottish Rite Freemason, intent on becoming active with our charities, of which the free Children's Learning Centers in all major cities in the Northern Jurisdiction is our most prominent. My very first jobs growing up were as a babysitter, both for neighbors and for cousins. I also umpired baseball for grade schoolers when I was in middle school. I taught at a few different daycare centers before, during, and after college, both in the suburbs and in the inner city (the former was actually more challenging!), and with kids of all ages, from infant to adolescent. My forte seemed to be with the pre-toddlers who were just forming their first words. There is little more exciting and rewarding than helping and watching pre-tods get all excited when they can point out something they see and know how to identify it verbally. They repeat the word with such empowered vigor, as if a single-word exclamatory sentence, every time they see the named object.

The Ancient Mystery Religions, of which Freemasonry is the modern vehicle, taught how knowing and invoking the correct name of something, including the various names of God, angels, and elements, gave one magical power over the thing being defined. And to paraphrase pioneer semanticist Alfred Korzybski, those who control symbols, control us. A good example is when Adam gave names to all the animals. In Freemasonry, the utterance of certain secret words broken up into syllables guards advancement through the degrees. Words create *ordo ab chaos*, "order out of chaos."

When toddlers get frustrated and lash out and cry, we tell them calmly to "Use their words." The articulated interpretation of otherwise ineffable phenomena give them that much more control over their situation. They are able to communicate with a better sense of understanding among others. At the last center I worked at, I gave special attention to a particular boy whose delay in oral language frustrated him to using his mouth for biting when it couldn't form the words he didn't know to speak. The parents were always impressed with how quickly their children were picking up and using new words under my guidance. It was all a matter of clear enunciation and repetition at any and every opportunity. When I would work with older students later, it seemed those struggling with speech issues were also often frustrated into physical misbehavior. Often they also seemed to be the first ones picking up and spreading "curse" words. The idea of a "curse" inherent in certain words reflects the magical power of words upon reality. You know I gave those troubled kids all freewriting journals and told them to just go nuts. And of course it was both the quiet ones and the frustrated, misunderstood "troublemakers" that really took up the pen like a sword or a magic wand, just as I had when I was young and confused and in need of a palette upon which to orchestrate my thoughts. It was really encouraging to see the conscientious metaphysical reflections that would surface between thought and expression, pen and paper, when the kids set quietly to writing.

Seeking a career in Special Education, I was recommended by a fellow CLC tutor to a charter school in the inner city of Milwaukee, co-founded by another alumni of the Masonic CLC program who struggled with Dyslexia herself. The school prides itself in using multi-sensory methods for children who learn differently. My fellow tutor from the CLC who recommended me there was their designated Orton-Gillingham pull-out specialist. So I can say that Masonry, through my involvement in its charity work, got me my first "real" job at 30 years-old. Hitherto I had worked at various daycare centers, hotels, greasy pizza joints, and microbreweries, trying to support myself as a self-published "starving artist," frequenting the open mic poetry scene with my off-beat Kerouakian jive. Being on salary for my first and only time gave me the chance to pay to self-publish my rather racy coming-of-age novels under a protective pseudonym, which with their experimental nature seemed otherwise unpublishable.

I didn't last too long at the "real" job. I was more than a bit overstressed, shuffling teaching, night classes, and tutoring at the CLC, and I wasn't used to so much busy organization and responsibility. Feeling still so young and a bit rebellious myself on top of that, it was difficult for me to find that fine line between friend and authority figure with my troublemaking protégé and all their various special needs, wild attention spans, and sensitive behaviors. Ironically or not, I somehow became the "mean teacher," perhaps because I could be too soft otherwise, and I got frustrated trying so hard just to teach, and not get trampled over. I was a new, young teacher still in pursuit of my license faced with up to fifteen students at a time of varying attention spans and learning disabilities, intermixed among 1st, 2nd, 3rd, 4th, and 5th grade, without much down time for prep, homework, or breathing. And I was usually alone because my paraprofessional took care of separate ability groups, which meant I was responsible for double the load of long-form lesson plans. It felt like 80% of my energy had to be spent on classroom management, and there was only that 20% left trying so desperately just to communicate enough through the storm to teach something. Lack of communicative control left me very frustrated on top of all the bureaucratic busywork that goes along with the special education field. I had come so far in life, but I was losing it.

Interestingly, my off-and-on girlfriend at the time, also an emotional poet, was beginning to find me passive-aggressive. There are different ways that the Written Word can help different people deal with their frustrations, whether one is a struggling reader/writer in the student's seat or an "expert" behind a teacher's desk or a poet's pen. It was right around the advent of text messaging, and she was frustrated by how much I preferred that over trying to explain myself verbally on the phone. My dad too always seemed to fumble over his words when he got frustrated with us, and as a sassy kid, I used to pick on him for it. But now I begin to think perhaps I too have a sort of verbal/social dyslexia ("dysverbia"?), and that may be why I compensate with/rely upon my great handle on the Written Word so much. I feel a certain comfortable security with my articulate control of the power of the Written Word. I will sometimes even avoid talking on the phone, getting into long conversations, especially with strangers, and social confrontations, for fear of feeling awkward or nervous, if I can just use email or text or a letter instead, in which realm I can get carried away on a long wind and feel that much more in control. I guess it's sort of the opposite issue of what someone with dyslexia encounters, and perhaps what makes my calling as a phonics tutor so natural. It might also explain why I struggled so much as a teacher, both with conveying concepts and keeping order, and why I wound up "yelling too much," as my boss would tell me. As someone who's always known to be so passive, easy-going, and soft-spoken, that came to me as a bit of a sobering shock; but perhaps that just goes to illustrate the frustration caused when there's a breakdown in communication. One of my favorite writers, the self-proclaimed "guerilla ontologist" Robert Anton Wilson (author of the *Illuminatus!* Trilogy) once stated that true communication only works between equals; in other words, On the Level.

I seem to do much better tutoring phonics one on one, where the setting is more conducive to working on more of a friendship level with my students and I only have to teach of my own only talent: language. Reflectively enough, what got me into Freemasonry was my passion for deciphering coded symbol systems.

I decided to use my newfound free time not just to finally catch up on my neglected free reading and writing (and being with the girlfriend), but also to further my influence with those struggling with reading and writing. I took up some new clients through a place called WILDD (Wisconsin Institute for Learning Disabilities/Dyslexia), the first of whom was a 7 year-old boy still struggling even to put his Alphabet together. I also began picking up hours tutoring privately. I had told my director at the CLC, Sara Pace, about my recent job loss and that I desperately wanted to pick up new clients to fill the void. I had already been thinking that what I really wanted to be doing was tutoring phonics one-on-one full-time. It seemed particularly comfortable and truly affective for me. If I could reach out to inspire at least just one student, and if that would make it all worth it, well then, it would be all the more effective if I could just focus on one student at a time. Unfortunately the budget was too tight to give me any more than the two students I already had at the CLC. But Sara had pointed me toward WILDD, which she had a hand in co-creating with Erv Carpenter, a Scottish Rite Freemason from the Valley of Madison. The Milwaukee branch of WILDD in West Allis was relatively new and just starting to take off under the directorship of Molly Brown. I was honored to be taken into the WILDD team in its inception and to be a part of its growth. Plans for reaching out to adult veterans as well as struggling children, with mathematics and written expression as well as phonics, and providing after school tutoring programs with Milwaukee Public Schools, were just beginning to take shape. But the budget at WILDD was even that much tighter than that of the CLC. In numerous ways, one can see how programs implementing the uniquely effective Orton-Gillingham method are sorely in need of both recognition and funding, just as the Education system and its struggling young protégé are sorely in need of the services and assistance such programs offer.

Further frustrating was the fact that just as I came begging for more clients, the two boys I'd been working with and developed a great comradery with at the CLC for over two years now had advanced under my wing to the point where I would have to pass them on to tutors who had had the more advanced training, which alas had not been available to me yet, also due to budget constraints. When later it seemed we had figured out a way to get the advanced training to those of us tutors who still needed it, through online courses, I received a disappointing email which put a sudden haulting curb on my short-lived relief: Apparently the advanced training course had so quickly filled up that I would again have to wait longer before I could be enrolled. I was told I would be in the "top ten" on the waiting list should anyone drop off. Eventually the advanced training would become more readily available through CD-ROM, but only after I already had to pass on my inceptive first two students as a tutor of phonics. Along with my passion for the calling, it was the personal commitment I had established to these two boys that kept me tutoring even as my schedule had been so stressfully overwhelmed on top of special ed. teaching and taking night classes toward my teacher's license.

With the first of the two boys I worked with, I shared a couple particular points of bonding: we both started out with long hair down to our shoulders, and we both had a great enthusiasm for baseball and the Milwaukee Brewers. As rewards after sessions, I would give him baseball cards I had collected when I was his age of players whose names fit with the particular spelling rules of each lesson. Once for each year I tutored him, I took him out to Miller Park for a ballgame as reward for mastering some particularly expansive sets of concepts. The second time around, all-star rightfielder Corey Hart had recently visited the boy's school through the Brewers' S.C.O.R.E. (School, Community, Opportunities, Role models, and Excellence) program. He was so overwhelmed by the presence of his hero that he had to go out to the hallway to catch his breath. Hart promised him that the next time he was at a ballgame, if he brought a big sign and his glove, he'd toss him a baseball. So we did just that. We went down along the right field fence just before the first inning, and got Hart's attention. Like a true professional role model in the community, Corey Hart recognized the boy and made true on his promise with a baseball tossed via the ballgirl. It was during Corey's particularly hot month of May in 2010 when he hit 13 home runs in 25 games. Suddenly other teams were showing great trade interest in Hart, but he was as dedicated to sticking with the Milwaukee community and contributing to his team as I was to sticking to my team with my talents as a tutor of phonics. But such dedication requires particularly unyielding commitment through tough trials and low points.

After such a hard-earned hot streak in the fall landing a big salary job and being more busy, successful, and responsible than I'd ever been used to before, spring had sprung with a series of swift blows, one after the other in a cold streak that left me discouraged and depressed. You don't even want to know how things played out with the girlfriend. Such bad luck continued into my summer. I even tried to go back to delivering pizzas, but alas my car stopped starting dependably. I would have to take the city bus everywhere I went tutoring. Not such a bad thing, because I would always get a lot of reading and writing done on the bus back in college. I even had my own inner city version of "The Wheels on the Bus," which I'd get friends to sing along with at poetry readings.

I took up some private tutoring at the West Allis Library with a boy whose sister was a student at the CLC. As WILDD continued to grow and the schoolyear came back around, I took up more and more clients, both children and adults. Before I knew it, I had eight different clients between the CLC, WILDD, and private practice, all between the ages of seven and twenty-five. I remember hearing once when I was just getting into the field through the CLC that one could make a complete and very decent living tutoring with Orton-Gillingham certification. Having set out more or less to do just that, things were falling into place according to plan and action, and now I can proudly say that I have done just that: I am a full-time tutor of the Orton-Gillingham method; it is my passion, my career, and my calling. And I have my own initiative and dedication to the field, and my enthusiasm for the language and interpretation of symbol-systems to thank, as well as the institution and philosophy of Scottish Rite Freemasonry, of which such initiative and service is emblematic.

It has been an interesting and inspiring transition and learning experience, especially as a former elementary teacher and a stubborn pacifist, now taking on adult military veterans of Iraq and Afghanistan as clients, on top of all the young children I tutor. The veterans are in the rewarding program at WILDD as a prerequisite part of their transition back into the job field and through college in order to receive their benefits. With one of my clients who served in Afghanistan, we have been reading through Dan Brown's newest book, *The Lost Symbol,* as part of our daily reading lesson. Reading this exciting and interesting book together on the edge of our seats has formed a great bond between an Afghanistan veteran struggling with phonics and a peace activist fiction writer tutoring phonics, as we uncover simultaneously the hidden keys to both the English language and the enigmatic adventure that is Freemasonry. Teaching literacy after all is perhaps the most appropriate and empowering way of recovering that fabled Lost Word so essentially citadel to the foundation and building of that great temple of Mankind dedicated to the GAOTU.

"In the beginning was the Word," states the introduction to the Gospel of John. And it is through its correct spelling and pronunciation, with a solid understanding of every letter which goes into it, that Man yields his creative genius effectively over the world around him. So teach the Ancient Mysteries toward the restoration of Fallen Man back to his original estate in God's own image.

Use your words. Know them, and use them wisely and honestly. They are the catalyst keys in Man's evolution from beast to God. This is the fruit of the Tree of Knowledge. So mote it be!

2 ~ The High Priestess
by Brother Tommy Baas

In designing my own Tarot deck, I chose to stay faithful to the standard conceptions of the Major Arcana (as embellished with my own personal interpretations & improvements), as have the great masters, because they are standards for a reason. The characters of these cards reflect in aspects actual figures existing in the archetypal realm (a parallel dimension of a higher density of elemental vibrations) who are very, very real, though, for this reason, whose attributes are too abstracted in myriad layers to be sensitively understand to us in our limited dimension in any other form but colorful mythological figures. Mythology, like ancient religions, as the chosen language of the Mystery Schools, surpasses any form of literature in its capacity to communicate simultaneously the highest philosophy, spirituality, and politics, all at once in images simple to understand. These archetypes captured in the Major Arcana are isomorphic in meaning with their correspondent numbers as well as their sephiroth on the kabbalic Tree of Life, which skeleton key is simultaneously an alphabetical and mathematical palette. And even as the Major Arcana of the Tarot have their counterparts in the Tree of Life, so too are they hidden symbolized for the vulgar in Moses's Ten Commandments. Not to mention the lines of the Sermon on the Mount, the Tribes of Israel, the Disciples of Christ, and of course the Zodiac. You might see at first glance that the four transposed letters on the book in the Priestess's right hand could seem to spell out Tarot (without the silent and invisible T), and indeed, no matter the order of which letters, words whose letters add up to the same value in the Kabbalah share the same meaning (and the Gnostics were right in associating the Knowledge-yielding serpent in Eden with Jesus), and of course the book in her right hand is none other than the Torah (without the silent H). Besides being written in the Kabbalic language, the Torah is the basis for the Old Testament, the text containing the story of Eden with the Tree of Life and the Tree of Knowledge, as well as the story of Moses with the Ten Commandments. The Tarot is simply the essence and meaning of the Torah (Old Testament) captured in colorful images and made a more practical oracle. And both are drawn out manifestations of the Tree of Life.

The High Priestess represents the Greater, Heavenly Garden of Eden (whereas the following card, the Empress, represents the Lesser, or Earthly Garden of Eden). She sits in her throne in the Temple of Solomon, as reflected in the standard Masonic temple, which was constructed to symbolically reflect the world in its every element. The floor of the Temple is tiled black and white (as has been echoed in the game of chess, also symbolic of the world), representing the constant interplay of dichotomies which pervades reality. So too do the pillars of Boaz (strength/beauty) and Jachin (establishment; "God establishes..."). On top of the Boaz pillar by her right hand, which holds the Torah (The Law of the Heavens) is the globe of the Heavens, the Celestial sphere. On top of the Jachin pillar by her left hand, which is offering the apple of Knowledge (of Duality, i.e. earthly knowledge) to man, is the globe of the Earth. Appropriately enough the Moon is between. The pillars also are important furniture of both Solomon's Temple and the Masonic Temple which is a re-creation of the same. A divergence I have chosen to make is to change them from temple pillars to armrests of the Priestess's throne, where they can be seen congruent with their symbolic equivalent on the temple of the human body, the legs, which are indeed our pillars of foundation. In this perspective we can see the orb of her tierra above and between as the Middle Pillar. In egg-like color and form as her royal crown, it symbolizes Venus, the planet commonly associated with the goddess and referred to in the Kabbalah as the Shekinah, by Light of which first and brightest star through a portal in the Temple an initiate is raised from spiritual death by the High Priestess, just as Isis to Osiris.

Another personal divergence made was to put the cross of Venus around her neck (between her breasts, also Two, though more pillows than pillars ;), where is, perhaps hastily errantly, typically pictured a regular Cross. Perhaps the old masters did not want to take anything away from the Empress, who also bears the cross of Venus. But it must be remembered that the Empress is indeed a lower, earthly manifestation of the Priestess, and so their symbols may be similar. The Venus cross is similar to the Egyptian Ankh often seen in the hand of Isis, who the High Priestess is a mythological equivalent of. These crosses symbolize rebirth. As well as the virgin mother and huntress Diana, the High Priestess could also correspond with the essence of both the Mother Virgin Mary and the Bride (or Courteson) Mary Magdalene, who each simultaneously reflect aspects of the Egyptian goddess Isis. The High Priestess is at once a symbol of the Virgin Birth and Fertility. Besides the floor design and the pillars, this card is full of symbols reflecting dichotomy. Like the shape and quantity of 1 reflects many aspects of the Magician, it is the same with the High Priestess and the number 2. Every little element is full of meaning in the esoteric world, each with layers of meaning decipherable according to the spiritual capacity and need of the interpreter. 2 is two 1's; in shape, like the pillars or the legs. Itself, the shape of 2 reflects the up-curling serpent in Eden who gave the apple of the Fruit of Knowledge of Good and Evil (i.e., knowledge of integral Duality) to Eve, who then offered it to her partner in duality, Adam. The apple in the Priestess's left hand is my own addition. The pomegranates on the wall of the Temple are standard, and were indeed well-represented by decoration in Solomon's Temple, as they are in Rosslyn Chapel. Actually the combination of these two sacred fruits make the most enchanting perfume brought out right by the pheromones of a priestess.

Two changes I made which I consider a real improvement upon the standards might be considered too "vulgar" for an image so sacred, but only to the deprived minds of the vulgar. Knowing the philosophy behind these symbols, it seems an atrocity if not a blasphemy that a few aspects here have been perhaps censored, deliberately or not, thus taking away from the profound meaning of the symbol. All descriptions of the High Priestess will tell you that she is clothed only in a dress of white light, yet every image appears materially clothed. I not only took the initiative to correct this discrepancy here, but I also made the light from the Sun which dresses also to penetrate her between the legs, just as the masculine Sun/Son does the feminine Earth/womb with life. And whereas the Moon, which the High Priestess is the very symbol of, is not even subtly passed off as in the sky in standard cards, but actually awkwardly positioned at her left foot, I once again took a "bold" initiative and placed the symbol of the moon where it belongs: over the female reproductive organ whose hormonal cycle reflects the Lunar Cycle. While we habitually consult our zodiacal Sun signs, it might do us each and all a service, whether as a woman or as a man trying to understand a woman, to consult the movements of our Moon signs.

To understand the Virgin Birth, contemplate the Source of that which makes you who you are from conception as distinct from each your father and mother or even the combined DNA of the two, yet is passed down through the mother, she being the receptor of the Holy Spirit. It is our soul which is the Christ or Logos within us, and this which like a perfect eternal flame is placed in our bodies at creation so to make us alive in Wisdom (Sophia) in a way that even our primate ancestors are not so Alive with a capital Alpha. So in this sense, which appropriately is the spiritual sense, the fundamentalists are right, just as are those who truly believe in the Grace of the Virgin Birth.

And just as it is the female who offers us such light of Wisdom, so too is it Eve who offers Adam the apple of Knowledge. The concepts are the same in meaning.

Taoism and Gnosticism, Eastern and Western religions respectively, yield characteristically dualistic philosophies. Reminiscent of the concept of the Virgin Birth, the Tao (the Way) works by the passive axiom, "Do by non-doing and all will be done." For feminine passivity of the High Priestess, this axiom takes on almost an opposite yet very similar meaning to the same phrase applied to the Magician, whose power is in his assertive will in alignment with that of the Cosmos.

And the Moon, of course, like the Vagina which takes in the phallus and by fertilization of dispelled seed recreates the child, yields its power by receptive reflection of active/solar/masculine power.

The camels on her throne represent Hebrew letter Gimel, meaning desert. And perhaps the way the camel carries its water in its hump across the desert is reflective of the concept of the Virgin Birth.

The bow and arrow at her left foot (a crescent where Rider-Waite puts the crescent of the Moon) reflects that, like Diana, she is a huntress.

In 1717 a governing authority known as the "Grand Lodge of England" was established at a meeting of four surviving lodges in the Apple Tree Tavern in London. Two Protestant clergymen, Dr. John Theophilus Desaguliers and Dr. James Anderson, were instrumental in setting up the self-styled governing body. Not all lodges were willing to submit to the rule of the new Grand Lodge, but by 1725 the original four lodges had grown to sixty four, of which fifty were in London. The Craft captured the fancy of certain members of the English aristocracy after 1721, and they in turn were flattered by the brethren. The first royal Grand Master took office in that year, and this position has since then been reserved to a nobleman.

-*Christianity and American Freemasonry*, William J. Whalen

The Apple-Tree
Art and Knowledge of the Craft

WINTER 2010   Volume I: Issue 4

Edited by Brother Tommy Baas, cover art from Courier & Ives, *The Tree of Temperance*
Freemasons Lodge #363, Milwaukee, WI

Art, essays, poetry, photography, etc., always welcome. Please submit all contributions to tbaas78@gmail.com

"Don't tell me there are no designs on the Trestleboard..."

Travel

Remove the earth from thy weary feet
to follow your compass home.
Up and down, to and fro
is now vanished like an ancient time.
The eternal progress of your Journey
Transcends outward motion
and frees your timeless soul
to a place lost by man many revolutions ago.
A lost word is of what they speak,
To be found another time
But this I say to you if you wish to truly know
That the word is not a word at all
But a sacred place you must go.

Brother Daniel Bast

Proper Instruction

Oh great pyramid of precision and strength
Beautiful and True
Man's architecture
does not design and create you.
Your golden grace is the hand of the Great Articifer
whose trestleboard drawings imbue the heart of men.
Lost to history or conscience the moon and stars give clue
to an ancient Temple Building we are all here to do.

Brother Daniel Bast

The Weather of Magic

This is the true weather of magic
Born of thermodynamics and the hydrologic realm
Magic cast down from the unseen
It is
The space between branches
The distance between waves
The time between seconds
The unfolding of frozen breath
The trance and pulse of wind whipping eyes,
burning through clothes
Passing through town and country
modeling our weary brow
This magic makes for heavy sleep.
This magic makes for heavy dreams.

Brother David J. White

A Winter Softly

Winter so quiet yet so fierce.
Side by side this is as it has
always been.
I will stay by your side if you
stay by mine.
Through the long nights we
rest heavy in thoughts filled
with ions and fractals.
The fractals coat the windows while we dream.
A winter softly as we rest asunder.
Branches heavy with ice.
Branches aloft in old sunlight.
A winter softly whispers
I still love you...

Brother David J. White

Thundersnow

The squalls move across the Great Lakes like
White Dragons from the north
Armed with cruel cyclonic breath they
thrash about waking old ghosts
from peaceful slumber
They once sent the steadfast masses of this northern
land into Windigo Psychosis
These Dragons leave no one spared
These Dragons stir long forgotten emotions
These Dragons cast spells of cold and lonesome
Like frozen dust
Like a blinding flash
Like horror from our ancient past
They watch and wait
and when you finally rest
their wings snap taut again

Brother David J. White

Ice

Black Ice
White Ice
Grey Ice
Ice Ice
Ice everywhere like a tiny universe of crushed light bulbs falling to Earth
The chill and the burn running through cloth and rubber and brick
Amazing how we humans have survived ice
Lived to to tell tales of Saber Toothed Tigers the size of horses
Wooly Mammoths the size of small whales with feet
Mountains of ice
Nothing but a vast remembrance of ice

Next time you are sipping a cocktail watching spirits
melt the ice stop and think how many ice ages have passed
How many will return

Brother David J. White

Cold and Dust

Cold and Dust
Blind by the sea and the crest.
Steel and the silver engines moan.
Daybreak ship shakes lonesome
afterthoughts dreaming of home.
Home fires burn in the fold.
Well wishers howl in the cold.
Salvation found on these rocky shores.
Badges worn for courage,
badges worn for honor,
badges worn for freedom,
badges worn for love.
All so children may quietly
sleep.

Brother David J. White

A Thousand Whispers

a thousand whispers
move through a thousand
trees and i can hear
the secrets of a thousand
ages

beauty lies in what magic
you can create with what
you hear
beauty lies in how you share
the whispers

Brother David J. White

Off season

every day on my way to work
I drive by the baseball stadium
on icy cold winter mornings before the sun
it's almost kind of sad
but reminds one at least
that the darkness is not forever
as a season ticket holder, it kind of feels like a second home—
at least a summer home
sometimes it seems they leave the roof open on random days off season
& just let the snow fall down on the field
I imagine it's covered by a huge tarp
or perhaps multiple large tarps
that probably lay there for 5 or 6 months out of the year
I imagine it's like a big flat blue cocoon
preserving season after season
the great American past time
for future times through all the presents
while we go shopping for starting pitching
& that forlorn fabled cure
for Midwestern Mediocrity
or at least winter—
what we call the off season

    -Brother Tommy Baas

Winter Wind

The song of the wind it blows bitter,
Across the white fields of blue,
The melody's one with the season,
The season of hardship and flu.

The rhyme of clear ice on the tree limbs,
Make a pattern of lace that is new,
It dazzles in sunshine with beauty,
But in dark is like ghosts of the few.

The black night it sparkles with diamonds,
Cold gem stones, both certain and true,
They sing of a time lost forever,
As with all of the Zodiac's crew.

The ice on the walkway, it beckons,
To a trap that one cannot but rue,
And ice is the totem of winter,
So watch for it ever anew.

The song of the wind it blows bitter,
If ever was bitterness true,
So head for the warmth of the taproom,
And an order of old fashioned brew!

      - *Brother Tom Curtis*

artwork by Tommy Baas

Jacob's Ladder
by Brother Derek Becker

The story of Jacob's ladder is a fascinating allegory found within the Book of Genesis, which explains the story of the vision of Jacob. Jacob was the son of Isaac, the son of Abraham whom was set to be sacrificed by Abraham as an offering to God, until God told Abraham that this was merely a test of his devotion. As the story goes, Jacob was traveling to Charan so that he could find a wife and also to escape the wrath of his brother Esau, after Jacob told his poor, starving brother that he would give him a bowl of soup in exchange for Esau's inheritance. While traveling, he stopped to rest under a tree and fell asleep, resting his head upon on a rock. Jacob then had a vision. A ladder appeared in front of Jacob, stretching from the Earth to Heaven. Angels were ascending and descending the steps of the ladder. The number of steps is unknown however several rabbinical commentaries claim that the angels each descend and re-ascend seven steps (Diamond 85). On top of the ladder was God, calling out to Jacob:

"I am the Lord, the God of your father Abraham and the God of Isaac. I will give you and your descendants the land on which you are lying. Your descendants will be like the dust of the earth, and you will spread out to the west and to the east, to the north and to the south. All peoples on earth will be blessed through you and your offspring. I am with you and will watch over you wherever you go, and I will bring you back to this land. I will not leave you until I have done what I have promised you. (Genesis 28:13-15)"

The allegory of Jacob's ladder has been interpreted time and again in an attempt to provide an illustration of the destiny of the Israelites. Some interpretations explain it as prophecy, considering it as the foreshadowing of the growth of the Israelites as a people and a nation. Others consider it a commentary that Jacob used to illustrate what he felt was his calling and destiny. We, as Free and Accepted Masons, interpret this story as providing moral lessons that are illustrated within the degrees. Whatever the interpretation, the allegory of Jacob's ladder provides an interesting insight into the development of both religion and ethics throughout the ages.

artwork by Tommy Baas

Maimonides' Interpretation

Famed Egyptian Jewish Rabbi, Maimonides, was esteemed for his profound influence on medicine, philosophy, and Kabbalah. His contributions to these areas are untranscended in their caliber. Without a doubt, Maimonides has had a profound impact upon the craft, even though Maimonides was never a Mason. Being a scholar of numerology and Kabbalah, Maimonides was able to provide an interesting insight into the allegory. The ladder itself, Maimonides interpreted, was symbolic of Mt. Sinai. As Moses ascended Mt. Sinai, upon which God sat, so did Jacob ascend the ladder he saw in his prophetic vision to meet God. God called down to Jacob from the top of the ladder and told Jacob that he had a calling to raise the Israelite nation; just as God called to Moses telling him that he has a calling to save the Israelite nation. The fact that Jacob envisioned a ladder rather than a staircase is considered to be a prognostication of the coming of Moses (Diamond 85). The Hebrew word for "ladder" is "sulam" (   ). The Hebrew writing of "Sinai" is " סיני ". Maimonides interpreted Jacob's vision to be prophetic of Moses' ascent, as whether written in English or Hebrew, the words "sulam" and "Sinai" both contain the same number of letters. Maimonides interpreted the numerology of these words, assigning a number corresponding to each letter in the alphabet representing the sequence in which it appears. When he did this, Maimonides found that the numerical value of both "   " and " סיני " are equal, both equaling 130. The significance of this being that Jacob is referred to in the Torah by two names, the first being "Jacob" and the second being "Yisrael". In the Torah, he is referred to as "Jacob" exactly 130 times. Also, Jacob's grandmother, Sarah, is known by two names. Sarah is called "Sarai" until God changes her name to "Sarah" (Genesis 17:15). After the point where God orders Abraham to refer to his wife as "Sarah" rather than "Sarai", Abraham is referred to in the five books of Moses exactly 130 times. In the book of Genesis, Adam was 130 Years old when he had his oldest son, Seth (Genesis 5:03). Maimonides put heavy stake in the numerology within the Torah, looking for parallels between writings as a means of explaining prophecy (Diamond 86).

Albert Pike 33° Interpretation

A second Interpretation is provided by our renowned and Illustrious Brother Albert Pike 33° in his famous work, "Morals and Dogma". Brother Pike argues that the ladder takes on a very different meaning. He argues that the ladder represents a pyramid, which may allude to the enslavement of the Israelites by the Egyptians. Pike argues that the Hebrew word "sulam" is derived from the root word "salal" which translates to "elevated" or "raised up". Also, "salalah" (which is derived from the same root word) means an "artificially made heap" which would allude to the pyramids of Egypt constructed by the Israelites (as there is no word in Hebrew which directly translates to "pyramid"). In this way, Jacob's dream could be a prophecy of the coming enslavement of the Israelites. Just as the ladder rose from the ground to reach heaven, so would the Israelites raise pyramids from the ground for the Egyptians. Pike also argues that pyramids of Egypt were built with seven levels to the pyramid. This would explain the seven steps the Angels were ascending and descending from as explained in rabbinical literature. This would mean that each step of the ladder would represent one level of the pyramid constructed by the Israelites (Pike 234).

Our Masonic Interpretation

We, as Free and Accepted Masons, interpret this story not as prophecy given to Jacob by God; but as an allegory, which provides an overwhelming amount of moral symbolism. First the ladder itself reaches from the Earth to Heaven symbolizing a connection between God and man. The ladder symbolized a connection between the terrestrial and the celestial and that both the earth and the heavens are intertwined and share a common bond with each other. The ladder is described as being grounded upon the Earth. This symbolizes that the connection between God and man will always be well grounded. As the ladder remains fastened to the ground, so will God remain fastened to the world. This also represents our strong faith and our dedication to our Grand Universal Architect. The ladder is strongly fastened to the ground just as our hope remains strongly fastened to our Deity.

One part of the story that is often overlooked is the rock that Jacob rests his head upon before his dream. The rock has taken on similar symbolism as the grounded ladder while at the same time takes on a similar symbolism of the grounded anchor. The rock symbolizes a well grounded hope and faith as well as strength and protection.

God has vowed to Jacob that the Israelites will never be abandoned by God and that the Israelite people will always be under the protection of God. The rock upon which Jacob is resting denotes protection, dedication, and hope that we may one day join the everlasting and the eternal. But why a ladder rather than a staircase? A ladder consists of three basic parts; one horizontal step connecting two vertical rungs. In the Entered Apprentice degree, these three parts of the ladder are taught to symbolize "Faith, Hope, & Charity". As taught in the Fellowcraft Degree, however, the number three takes on a different meaning. The allegory is reconstructed in this degree as the ladder is represented by a winding staircase, consisting of three, five, and seven steps. Each of these are an odd number of steps so when one advances up the staircase, the first foot to leave the ground is the same foot to reach the top step. The staircase taken as a whole, totals fifteen steps, just as in the fifteen individuals originally involved in the plot explained in the Master Mason Degree (twelve of whom recanted, thus leaving three). Fifteen is also representative of the Tetragrammaton, which is the ineffable name of God, as the Hebrew numbers 10 and 5 together are numerically equivalent to the unspeakable name of Deity. As well, the number 10 is representative of the Universe. The number 10 is the first number that encompasses all of the single digit numbers just as the universe encompasses all. 10 also represents completion as it finalizes the single digit numbers and begins the first new cycle of numbers. 5 represents balance as it is at the center of the single digit numbers. As 10 represents the universe and completion and 5 represents balance, 15 would be representative of the perfectly balanced and complete Universe that was so well designed by the Great Architect. The staircase is a path of fifteen steps, each step representing another step of virtue toward knowledge of our Architect who drafted our perfectly balanced universe.

The first three steps are taught to represent the three principal officers of the lodge; Worshipful Master and the Junior and Senior Wardens (the symbols of which are the square, level, and plumb, denoting, virtue, equality, and integrity). But the number three, remember, represents so much more in Masonry. We have three great lights illuminated by three lesser. The sun has three main positions appearing in the East, South, and West. Humans are said to have three basic parts; the physical, the intellectual, and the spiritual/emotional. The intellectual and the spiritual are both represented by the vertical rungs of the ladder (the intellectual and spiritual being the parts of the human to reach the heavens), as they are held together by the physical part of humans until they reach their destination. The number three also represents the three main parts of the earth; the land, the oceans, and the sky.

The next five steps of the ladder are said to represent the five types of design used in architecture; Tuscan, Doric, Ionic, Corinthian, and Composite. These are taught to represent the five senses, Hearing, Seeing, Feeling, Smelling, and Tasting. But what else does this represent? According to Pythagoras, the number five represented justice, equality, and balance because, remember, five occurs in the center of the single digit numbers, just as the five steps appear in the center of the winding staircase.

The next seven steps are taught to represent the seven areas of study; Grammar, Rhetoric, Logic, Arithmetic, Geometry, Music, and Astronomy (Geometry falling as the fifth step representing universal balance). These seven steps parallel the seven steps ascended and descended by the angels in Jacob's vision. Within Masonry, the number seven also represents the line of officers; Junior and Senior Stewards, Junior and Senior Deacons, Junior and Senior Wardens, and the Worshipful Master. We have seven working tools; the common gavel, the 24 inch gauge, the square, the level, the plumb, the compasses, and the trowel. The letter "G" is the seventh letter of the alphabet. It is said that the world was created in seven days. When the Israelites sieged the city of Jericho with the Arc of the Covenant, the siege lasted seven days. The city was circled seven times on the seventh day of the siege. Every time the city was circled seven trumpets made from ram horns were blown seven times (Joshua 6:01-27).

There are many interpretations of Jacob's vision that each has their own unique way of illustrating different aspects of life. The allegory can be used to illustrate times such as the enslavement of the Jews by the Egyptians and it can also be seen to have prophesized the coming of Moses to lead the Israelites out of Egypt. We, as Free and Accepted Masons, use the allegory to express moral lessons of how to live a decent life in union with our fellow man. Jacob's vision can be used to illustrate areas that span all realms of belief and ethics. Maybe the most important concept of Jacob's vision is that it knows no bounds and can be used to illustrate so many areas, showing that everything is so interconnected within that Universe which was designed by our revered Grand and Supreme Architect.

Works Cited

Diamond, James (2002). *Maimonides and the Hermeneutics of Concealment: Deciphering Scripture and Midrash in the Guide of the Perplexed.* Albany, NY. State University New York Press

Pike, Albert (2002). *Morals and Dogma of the Ancient and Accepted Scottish Rite Freemasonry.* Kessinger Publishing, LLC.

Jacob's Ladder   ~   by Tommy Baas

Pardon the imperfect photography; the painting is part of an immense mural I had done in my dad's basement, not longer after I was raised. Unfortunately, it has since been painted over.

Required Reading

Albert Pike's *Morals and Dogma*

From Brother Damon Sanchez

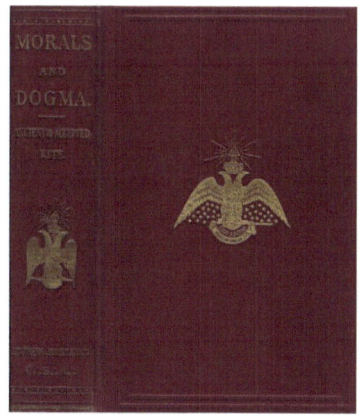

My favorite section of the text is located in the 28th degree:

The World or Universe was thus compared to man: the Principle of Life that moves it, to that which moves man; the Soul of the World to that of man. Therefore Pythagoras called man a microcosm, or little world, as possessing in miniature all the qualities found on a great scale in the Universe; by his reason and intelligence partaking of the Divine Nature: and by his faculty of changing aliments into other substances, of growing, and reproducing himself, partaking of elementary Nature. Thus he made the Universe a great intelligent Being, like man--an immense Deity, having in itself, what man has in himself, movement, life, and intelligence, and besides, a perpetuity of existence, which man has not; and, as having in itself perpetuity of movement and life, therefore the Supreme Cause of all.

Like a lot of Hermetical texts of the day, Pike brings forth the concept of finding reflections of the Macro Universe in the Micro Natures of man. What I've found in general the Macro/Micro concept is typically wrapped around aspects of Male and Female, Good and Evil and Mathematical similarities, Polarity etc.

But what I found different about Pike's take on this was the idea of linking Man to God through movement, life and the perpetuity of existence. Which I guess you could say carries within it basic elements of Male and Female, etc... But what made this profound was how it elegantly explained that life exists through its own perpetuity. We choose to exist, therefore we perpetuate...

Editor's note ~ For the next issue, let's look at Manly P. Hall's *Secret Teachings of All Ages*. It's a pretty awesome compendium of knowledge, to say the least. If you haven't read it yet, pick it up now and let us know what you think. And if you have read it, well, do the same! Hopefully with the next installment of "Required Reading" in the Spring, we'll get more responses, and hopefully I'll even make the time to write up one myself. Thank you, Brother Sanchez, for this insightful contribution, and single-handedly making sure this new segment of the *Apple-Tree* gets off the ground catches on!
-Tommy Baas

3 ~ The Empress

from the Turtle Tarot, by Tommy Baas

Each card derives meaning through perspective in how it relates to other cards. In general, where each falls in numerical order (and more especially value), and relative to where it falls in a reading. Symbolizing the "Lesser" Eden (earthly) or "Lesser" Eve (human female), naturally the Empress will have characteristics similar to, yet more mundane than the High Priestess. And of course being the Empress, it will be seen that she shares similar but appropriately opposite counterpart characteristics to her consort, the Emperor.

Like The High Priestess, she bears the same Ankh-like cross around her neck. But she is actually ruled by this star, whereas the High Priestess is ruled by the Moon. Whereas the Moon was shown over the HP's womb where her power is impregnated, the ruling power of the Empress has now moved up her pregnant belly, in that same cross hanging between her fully developed breasts. The Empress is also a symbol of fertility, and the abundance of vegetation growing around her and the rabbit running through it reflect this. But her birthing is not so immaculate, and she must show her pregnancy in her full belly and endure the pains of labor. So the Empress symbolizes both abundance and the great sacrificial strength of the receptive woman. She is not a huntress like the High Priestess who seeks out the right man to make child with, but rather she is one fully immersed in the processes of Nature which make up her kingdom, Eden on Earth, taking on the cycles of life as her own. It is quite fitting that the cross resting on her pregnant belly symbolizes Life itself. And like her belly, the Moon in the sky shining down on her is full. It almost looks like a Harvest Moon, and this could be reflected in the ripeness of vegetation all around. Harvest time comes when the vegetation is fully developed and ready to be picked for consumption, before all else in nature otherwise dies or hibernates and the cycle of life continues. It occurs in Autumn, the "Fall" from Eden, which is Summer when all is most alive in Nature. But knowing the cycle of Life as taught us by the cycle of the seasons, we know that every fall occurs only that we might rise again later all the more evolved after winter, which is like a natural death. The ancients used the symbols of Nature in their mythologies, since it is the most obvious and evident way to teach the immortality of the soul and the reaping reincarnation of the fruits of dispelled seeds sewn.

The Empress is the vehicle for and symbol of regeneration. Note in the forest here especially the evergreens, symbols of eternal life, the sunflower (the one image of the sun present in this card, and the one sun that is out even at night), and the rows of corn which in shape double as the Fleur de Lis-- the flower sacred in France to the Merovingian bloodline and the Priory of Sion which protects it. Their militant branch, the Knights Templar, have for this interest the chivalric duty of reverently protecting the Daughter in LAW of the Virgin Mary, the holy temple concubine and bride of the Christ, Mary Magdalene. It is the Magdala, earthly pregnant with the Christ's son, who she must hide from persecutors striving to hide the esoteric side of religion, that the Empress represents like the Virgin Mother.

The stars around the Moon number twelve, that of the zodiacs, disciples of Jesus, Tribes of Israel, and hours on a clock. Regarding Time in terms of pregnancy, we think generally of nine (which is her card's numerical value) months. But a woman knows it is actually ten months, and the first few months are an essential development time for the child when it is more or less still attached to the mother, while maybe not technically inside her. The Empress is also crowned for her royal position in the evolution of Mankind with a diadem of twelve stars above her tierra of roses, for from her womb come men of all twelve zodiacs, tribes, and times. For this, she is at once the brotherhood of man's mother, sister, daughter, and lover. She is the second syllable He in the Tetragrammaton (Yod He Vauv He; YHVH; Jehovah), whereas the High Priestess is the first, and likewise she is the womb that is the element of Earth, whereas the HP is the womb which is the element of Air that reaps her seeds in the wind.

And what of the apple of Knowledge that the High Priestess, the goddess who procreates with human men, offered to him as a lesson in the nature of Duality? Said human man, the Goddess's lover taken from her by the jealous God which created him, now hangs for their sin from the very Tree of Knowledge from which the "bad" apple fell. He is the Hanged Man who appears later in the deck, but as you'll see we could just as well call him the well-hung Man, and perhaps it is from his own umbilical chord which he hangs here from his Family Tree. His line of blood drips into the river running through the valley, call it the Nile or the Jordan or the Red Sea of menstrual blood or his DNA through sperm seeping into her uterus. You see here that the river stops right between her legs, as if feeding into the ocean that is her fertile womb. And soon the dam will break and so will her water, like rain upon the vegetation beneath her dress. It should be noted that while the HP was clothed only in a dress of white light from the Sun (which also, in reflecting off the Moon of her womb, impregnated her with S(o/u)n of God), the Empress, like Eve after having eaten the apple knowing herself naked, is actually materially clothed. Still she wears white, for having sewn her own garments with the silk procured for her by her hunting human man, she likewise makes her own purity. And in the words of William Blake, "The Soul of Sweet Delight can nev'r be defil'd." As the High Priestess sits surrounded by pomegranates decorated on the walls around her, the Empress has sewn this same fruitful symbol into her only "walls" outside in nature, her dress. Around her bees with their stingers buzz around for honey to bring to the Queen. The staff of the Empress is of purple royalty.

It was an act of assertive pride that made the earthly Adam eat the apple (know that he also has a heavenly doppelganger) when offered it by Eve (who having bit it first already went from heavenly to earthly, for that was the only way she could physically make love to an earthly man, as the Knowledge yielding serpent, his phallus, had tempted her to).
Naturally earthly man wanted to impress this woman come down from Heaven, and was told by his serpent that the psychedelic aphrodisiac could make him like a god himself, able to discern between Good and Evil, and to live forever.

As we all know the story goes, the ingesting of the Knowledge of the abstractly complex concepts of Right and Wrong would be man's undoing. Though in the words of St. Thomas Aquainas, it would also eventually prove his "felix culpa," or happy accident, since by the power of Freewill granted by this newfound ability to balance opposites, man would through maturity evolve to godhood of his own accord, by the sweat of his brow and the work of his two hands, once he had through much trial and error learned to balance his thoughts with his actions. East of Eden, you learn quickly that if you can't control your temptations and emotions or your words when emotions get the best of you, if you can't take a positive approach from a seemingly dark foreshadowing and churn negative energy into a positive outcome, if you either think you're completely a victim of Fate or completely a Master of it, rather than one by will in constant conversation with it, then you should not be messing with occult knowledge, for your own sake and for that of others. Thus it is guarded with rigorous tests of morality.

Much knowledge can and should be studied alone, but to paraphrase Bruce Springsteen, "Individual freedom [or knowledge] in and of itself without the bonds of society of friends, family, and love, ends up feeling pretty meaningless." Most people immersed in the Occult are indeed simply searching for real Connection. Man and woman, integral opposites themselves, were given each other to figure out the secrets together. Each can learn much of their own gender's Nature alone, but such will get lonesome and seem meaningless, and one will constantly be craving what can be learned of the other until through dating and procreating and then discussing the Cosmos in the Afterglow, they can complement each other in an alchemical marriage. This is the Great Work.

Resting on her pregnant belly, the Empress holds the Grail, that prize of all religion, which she is and bears and drinks from. It is the wine alchemically made of the blood of the sacrificed savior of Mankind, who died for our sins that we might like him too become like gods ourselves and live forever. She is the woman protected by the Knights Templar (guardians of the Grail) who bears within her the remaining blood of the savior, and churned to merlot by the winepress of her thighs, it is she who can dispense it to those worthy, she who can comfort Fallen Man in his loneliness, she who can share her abundance of Life with all, nurturing with compassion and understanding, feeding with warm milk from her breasts, she from whose womb continues the bloodline of the Christ. She holds the future of Mankind in her belly, which is hers and the Son of Man's child, Christ's resurrected Self. And she is the Black Madonna, forsaken and shunned by the Orthodox jealous Creator God, who as Samuel or Ialdaboath is a bastard child born of an even higher God who procreated with a lower angel woman, and He Himself fornicates with earthly women like the Virgin Mary (mother of the Son of Man and mother in LAW of the Empress), and this explains his violent jealousy and insecure desire to be the "only" god. The Empress, similar in this way to the prostitute or stripper, who by the patriarchal society is shunned, pimped out, and fondled, remains an unconditional friend and savior to all Fallen human men East of Eden, particularly humble knights and those troubled. She is their patron saint, both maternal and as a lover. As is the pervading concept of this card, it is by the grace of her Love that man dies of his lower nature and is reborn into his higher nature. In other words, she takes boys and makes them men.

A prominent symbol of the Order of the Rose-Croix, the pelican to her right symbolizes this sacrificial abundant nurturing in how she plucks blood of her own breast to feed her seven baby birds with. Their eggs, like the Ishtar bunny and the Full Moon (lune, loony, lunar), symbolize fertility. The pelican could also be interpreted as a stork, which of course would fit mythologically with childbirth.

A prominent symbol of the Scottish Rite of Freemasonry, and the most ancient of all symbols derived from the Egyptians, the double-headed phoenix is seen on her heart-shaped (denoting love and life, double-breasted, like the shape of her number 3) shield to her right. Even before Freemasonry was the citadel which sparked the Republic of America, this symbol was mistakenly expressed as a double eagle, and the blunder is still utilized today. Historically, it represents the conjoining of two opposites or kingdoms, though still maintaining two heads. In government this can be interpreted as Democrat and Republican, in sex as male and female, and in Masonic legend as either King Solomon and Hiram King of Tyre or Zerrubabel and King Darius. The Phoenix is known to use sprigs of acacia in building its nest, the same which are placed over the grave of the martyred Hiram Abiff in the Masonic legend, and like the evergreen decorated at Christmas, symbolizes eternal life. To the ancients the phoenix was an appropriate symbol of the immortality of the human soul since, like the reincarnated spiritual nature of man from its physical bodies, it is reborn of its own dead Seven times Seven times. It has been suggested that not only should the eagle of Masonic symbolism be a phoenix, but so should the pelican, who indeed plucks of itself to feed its Seven new lives.

Within one's individual life, one goes through many Seven-year cycles of complete cellular regeneration, at the end of each which one is comprised of a whole new set of cells, and so becomes basically a whole new person. Seven too is the number of the Chakras within us which we must in succession excite so to come to our pre-blueprinted evolved godhood. These steps are also reflected in the seven days of "Creation" and the Seven "Churches" of Asia (Assiah = rising up).

The Hebrew letter of the Empress, Daleth, fittingly refers to a door.

TOMMY'S TURTLE TAROT DECK, 2008

Brothers

We're very much the same
But that's not at all
how we came
I know he could very well
be my best friend
The only friend that would
be there to the end
We used to fight and
Cause a lot of fuss
That was part of growing up
just the two of us
Now we're older and I know
I caused a lot of pain
Now I hope he can put it
behind him just the same
I really regret what I did in the past
I hope our friendship as brothers
through time will last

Nicholas Rozanski, 1975 – 2010, stepson to Brother Jim Bacon

www.ingramcontent.com/pod-product-compliance
Lightning Source LLC
Chambersburg PA
CBHW041403020526
44115CB00036B/13